YOU'LL NEVER BELIEVE ME

ABOUT THE AUTHOR

Kari Ferrell is a producer, writer, speaker, activist and creator who achieved notoriety in the mid-2000s as the 'Hipster Grifter'. She now focuses on work around incarceration and the justice system, mental health and human rights, and runs her own production company, Without Wax. When she's not doing the above, she enjoys spending time with her partner and rescue pup, solving crossword puzzles, eating, boxing (to counteract the eating), getting stoned and writing about herself in the third person.

YOU'LL NEVER BELIEVE ME

*A LIFE OF LIES, SECOND TRIES, AND
THINGS I SHOULD ONLY TELL
MY THERAPIST*

KARI FERRELL

CORONET

First published in the United States by St. Martin's Press,
an imprint of St. Martin's Publishing Group
First published in Great Britain in 2025 by Coronet
An imprint of Hodder & Stoughton Limited
An Hachette UK company

1

Designed by Gabriel Guma

A CIP catalogue record for this title is available from the British Library

Hardback ISBN 9781399719933
Trade Paperback ISBN 9781399719940
ebook ISBN 9781399719964

Typeset in Adobe Caslon Pro

Printed and bound in Great Britain by Clays Ltd, Elcograf S.p.A.

Hodder & Stoughton policy is to use papers that are natural, renewable
and recyclable products and made from wood grown in sustainable forests.
The logging and manufacturing processes are expected to conform
to the environmental regulations of the country of origin.

Hodder & Stoughton Limited
Carmelite House
50 Victoria Embankment
London EC4Y 0DZ

The authorised representative in the EEA is Hachette Ireland, 8 Castlecourt
Centre, Dublin 15, D15 XTP3, Ireland (email: info@hbgi.ie)

www.hodder.co.uk

There may be easier ways to self-improvement,
but sometimes it happens that the shortest distance
between two points is a crooked line.
—*The Twilight Zone*

CONTENTS

YOU'LL NEVER BELIEVE ME

ADOPT DON'T SHOP

"Why is your face so flat?"

"Why didn't your *real* parents want you?"

The words hurtled at me with all the force of a speeding rubber bullet, meant to hurt but not completely maim. No, my attacker wanted to keep me alive long enough to flog me, too.

The other first graders had gathered around me and my interrogator on the playground, like curious cows coming from miles away as soon as they heard the slightest bellow.

"My parents *chose* me, yours just made a mistake," I fired back.

My pint-sized peers immediately let out a series of loud, satisfied oohs and aahs. While some of them had pointed accusatory fingers at me seconds ago—as if I were guilty of a crime, the grand offense of being The Other—I watched as they pivoted and turned against my attacker. The smug smile disappeared from his face and his cheeks burned red, and at that very moment I realized that my secret weapon was my words. And to a much larger extent, my mouth (but that would *really* come in handy many years later).

As we shuffled back into the classroom and sat down for show-and-tell, I remember feeling like I was in the midst of a blizzard—I couldn't look in any direction without seeing a blanket of white faces. I was the only Asian in my class—one of two in the entire school—and I was used to standing out and being on display when all I wanted was to blend in.

My teacher, Mrs. Adams, called my name and I walked to the front of the classroom. I sighed impatiently to myself (and likely to everyone else, as well) as I waited for Ryan Anderson to stuff his dad's stupid baseball cards into his Aladdin backpack.

Finally, the stage was all mine! I stepped carefully, dramatically; one slightly pigeon-toed foot in front of the other. My *Tiny Toon Adventures* high-top sneakers squeaked and creaked, announcing my arrival with every step. I was clutching a small item in my hand and I was ready to blow some goddamn minds.

"You all know me as Kari, which is who I'm known as when I'm in my *human form* . . ."

Pause for dramatic effect.

"But in reality I'm actually an alien from another planet, and when I was a baby I was cursed and trapped in this body for one hundred years."

Some of the kids laughed while others looked curious—I focused on them, looking straight into their eyes as I opened my hand and revealed an ID card. Mrs. Adams looked amused, a curious smile playing across her lips. Like a deranged three-foot QVC model, I waved my fingers around it and pointed at the words imprinted on the card: LEGAL RESIDENT ALIEN.

Mrs. Adams's smile disappeared and was replaced with concern.

"Ohhh, so that's why your face is so flat. You crashed your spaceship because you couldn't see out of your slanty eyes," I heard a kid say.

"Andy! That's enough!" shouted Mrs. Adams.

As I plummeted back down to earth by the heat of my embarrassment, I mumbled a thanks and walked back to my seat, determined not to give stupid Andy Swanson and his merry band of buttheads the satisfaction of seeing the tears well up in my allegedly inferior eyes.

These kids may have been cruel, but they brought up questions that I also wanted the answers to.

My *Coming to America* origin story was limited: I was born in Jeollabuk-do, a province in the southwestern part of South Korea roughly twice the size of Rhode Island. Most people can pinpoint the town they were born in, if not down to the specific hospital, but for me it was simply another unknown on a long list of unknowns. My birth parents were poor and couldn't afford to take care of me and wanted to give me a better life. I got that better life when I was shipped off to America at five months old. The end.

The thing is, I truly do believe that I got a better life. My childhood was one of happiness, joy, and so, so much love. But the fact of the matter is that my parents were raising a kid who needed a lot of "special attention," all while still being kids themselves.

Karen and Terry (= Kari, get it?), were high school sweethearts who married young, as was common in 1970s Phoenix, Arizona. My mom came from an upper-middle-class family—all manicured lawns and front rooms you weren't allowed to sit in—and my dad was born to self-identifying hillbillies from Kentucky— all trailer parks in the middle of nowhere and milk in beer bottles.

When my mom was younger, a doctor told her that her life-giving parts, the things that make a woman a woman (as far as antiquated thinking went), were sabotaging her and that she wouldn't be able to get pregnant. Somewhere down the line, my parents realized that giving actual birth was only a small part of being a parent, and so they decided to embark on the tumultuous and often heartbreaking process of adopting a baby from overseas.

I've never asked them why they chose South Korea specifically. Did they want everyone to know that I was adopted from the get-go? There would never be an instance where I'd be mistaken for their biological kid (unlike my younger brother, adopted when I was eight years old, who is half white, half Mexican, and as a kid had an uncanny resemblance to my dad). Was it like choosing a puppy based on how cute they were? Were they adopting me or rescuing me or both? Did they know what they were getting into?

For better or worse, my mom and dad never treated me like I was anything but exactly like them. By all accounts, I *was* very

American. My favorite bands growing up were the Monkees, the Mamas & the Papas, and Fleetwood Mac—vestiges of my dad's former life as a long-haired hippie. My favorite TV shows were *The Dukes of Hazzard* and *The Wonder Years*. What's more goddamn American than that?

To be fair, the Asian erasure wasn't due to a total lack of trying on my parents' part. I recall being asked when I was four or five years old if I wanted to learn more about my motherland, and my response was that *this*, the United States, was my home. I don't remember being asked about it again.

My parents did a wonderful job raising me considering the resources available to them. This was decades before Reddit, Quora, and myriad websites dedicated to transracial/transnational adoption. My mom and dad—like *all* moms and dads of the time—were going off gut instinct and the intense drive to be better parents than their own. There was no playbook, and God knows they could have used one, because I certainly wasn't an easy child. For as well-behaved as I was, my neediness knew no bounds. I always felt safe, but there was a constant fear living inside me that something bad was going to happen to my family.

At night, lying in bed while my dad sat in a rocking chair next to me (I would wail in panic if he wasn't there), my fists balled up tight, I'd wait for my mom to get home from her late shift at the Old Country Buffet. I'd count the seconds until I heard our garage door open, signaling to my brain that I could finally rest easy. Yet, despite my complete and desperate yearning for my mom, my poor, fucked-up, stress-addled baby brain would deliver completely devastating lines to her as she came into my bedroom to tuck me in and kiss me goodnight, like: *"My heart says I love you, but my mind says I hate you."* I mean, Jesus Christ, what do you even do with that as a parent? For as many nights as I spent crying and praying for understanding, I wonder how often my mom and dad were doing the same.

People around me often speculated about why I was "abandoned." As in, they would ask me—a child—why I wasn't worthy of a family. I had a prepared answer in my back pocket, ready to go: "I'm adopted, which means that God loved me so much that he knew I should be with my mom and dad, even if they weren't the ones who had me."

These kinds of questions were asked mostly by kids, but you'd be surprised by the weird, racist, ignorant shit that came out of adults' mouths, too.

I vividly remember sitting in a cart at the grocery store, my mom close by, grabbing all the saturated fats off the shelf—snacks that had so much sugar they made your teeth vibrate—and anything that was advertised as being "x-treme" (which was basically everything). A woman farther down the aisle who was standing in front of the bagged cholesterol glanced first at my mom and then at me, and smiled as she bounded toward us.

"Ohhhhh my gosh! What a beautiful child! Is she yours?"

Without missing a beat my mom responded by telling her my name and that I was adopted from South Korea. (Always "adopted," never "born in.")

A smile still plastered across the woman's very pale face, she leaned over to me and said, "You must be so grateful that your parents *saved you*." I nodded eagerly—of course I was grateful! Wait, was it an option to not be?

There's no doubt in my mind that this overzealous lady was earnest and meant no ill will. Maybe she even recounted the day's events to her own family that night over dinner—their genetically similar smiles grinning back at her. Whatever the case, this woman, and many others like her, have sent me into a tailspin more than once. I often wonder what she thought my parents were saving me from. The mental image in her uncultured brain was likely similar to the image in my four-year-old one: rice paddy fields, dirt floors, no TVs or shopping malls or flush toilets.

I didn't realize until much later in life that 1990s Korea had one of the largest nominal GDPs in the world—and still does—and was integral to the internet revolution and modern-day life as we know it. Were my parents *saving* me from becoming an obsessive gamer, dying in a cyber cafe because I wouldn't get up to take a piss? Thanks, I guess?

But none of this mattered back then. And quite frankly, it mattered the least to me. I accepted the cards that I was dealt. It was a winning hand, after all.

Or maybe it did matter. I was always second-guessing myself. I got so good at shoving my confusion deep down into my body that I was like a competitive hot dog eater, dipping the buns in water so they're more palatable, so I could cram and cram and cram. I was processed meat trying to process me. My identity, my place, my reality—why couldn't I figure any of this out? Cram, cram, cram.

All of this might have been easier to sort through if I had a community to fall back on. If I could come home after school and hear my aunties complain about how they, too, were asked if they were going to eat the family dog for dinner, maybe then I could have started to crack the ethnic enigma that was my general existence. But I didn't have that, so I didn't talk about any of it with anyone.

And honestly, when I was at home, the adoration of my parents seemed to soothe and heal all of my invisible wounds. They absolutely cherished me, and I felt their love on a deep level. We were a very affectionate family, and my close relationship with my mom and dad manifested itself in a lot of hugs and kisses, and also by being spoiled as shit.

I was given anything and everything I ever asked for and then some. Maximalism was one of the main tenets of my childhood. We expressed our emotions through possessions, and under the heavy hand of post-recession capitalism it didn't matter whether we had the means to afford them. Happy? Buy some shit. Sad? Buy some shit. Indifferent? Buy some shit! Layaway was our love language. Post-dated checks were our proof of passion—so much so that I never suspected that we were poor. There were signs, of course, but to my mom and dad's credit (or lack thereof, har har) they dampened the blow by making sure we always had the name-brand snacks and wanted for nothing. I didn't know that a grocery store produce manager and a waitress shouldn't have been able to afford all of the things we had.

In the summer of 1992, we had a garage sale and one of the items up for grabs was our laughably large VHS camcorder. (If love isn't hauling that thing around Disneyland on your shoulders to capture all the magic moments, I don't know what is). I don't remember how much it sold for, but I do remember the feeling of despair that filled the car and my mom's tears streaming down her face after she tried to cash the man's bounced check. I was sad for us, angry at the man, and confused that you could simply lie about having the money to buy something and still get to keep it.

A pivotal moment in my life, I'm sure of it.

Though these gutting moments stand out in my memories, building up like plaque in a meth mouth, most of the time I was living it up in my themed bedroom (various iterations throughout the years) chock-full of toys, stuffed animals, and oh so many books. The first true love of my life, books, were my solace and my sanctuary (not to be dramatic or anything). I was reading at a high school level by age five and fucking murdered every Pizza Hut Book It! reading challenge presented. It's still a personal point of pride that I got to treat my class to a pizza party not once, but thrice.

My fellow classmates appreciated my smarts because they benefited from them, but I never felt like they appreciated *me*. By the fifth straight recess playing a self-deprecating game of Simon Says, I knew it was true.

"CHINESE!" *eyes pulled to an upward slant*

"JAPANESE!" *eyes pulled to a downward slant*

"DIRTY KNEES!" *points at knees*

"LOOK AT THESE!" *points to chest*

Alanna Briggs, the most popular girl in my class (her mom let her wear lip gloss in the first grade because she had a developmentally disabled younger brother who took up all their parents' bandwidth; and she certainly was on her way to becoming a hussy, if the ladies I overheard at church were to be believed), had learned the chant from her cousin over the summer, and she brought it back to Silver Hills Elementary. I went along with it, because it's better to die with your tribe than on your own, waiting for the buzzards to pick you off by the monkey bars.

But even now, looking back at these moments that caused me such deep-seated pain, it's hard to blame my classmates. They didn't know that I was moderately-okay-to-good-looking depending on the day because they had never seen someone with my face, so they called me ugly. They didn't know East Asia isn't just China, so they called me a chink. (I would have preferred the much more breed-specific zipperhead. Like, if you're gonna call me a slur, let's not be lazy about it, okay?)

Some may see my obliviousness as a blessing bestowed upon me by our Lord and Savior, Jesus Christ, a protective shield in the form of *ignorance is bliss*. And while I have to agree that at the time that mindset may have served me well, in my adolescence it threw me for a fucking loop and took me for a ride. The people around me didn't know their actions would affect me in ways that would bring forth utter chaos and disaster, or that many of them who started as friends would end up as victims.

And neither did I.

2

LET'S GET CELESTIAL

Beads of sweat ran down my brow as a group of grown men in suits encircled me, my stomach doing flips as their arms extended toward the chair I sat in, advancing like wolves who had singled out a sickly fawn. I shuddered and tried very hard to stay still.

A small bottle of yellow ointment was held above my head. I felt the cool drops seep into my scalp and then the weight of ten hands upon me.

"Kari Michelle Ferrell, I am anointing you by the authority of the Melchizedek Priesthood of the Church of Latter-day Saints. The oil placed upon you has been consecrated to heal those who are sick and afflicted."

I coughed loudly, my five-year-old body racked with pain. Some of the men turned their heads away from me. I had a contagious viral infection called, pointedly, hand, foot, and mouth disease, the hallmark of which was awful, tender sores on the namesake areas.

"Lord, please bless this child, who is pure in her intentions and committed to walk the path of righteousness as the Holy Spirit directs," Bishop Fowler droned on. For being possessed by such a powerful entity, he sure sounded bored as shit. He might as well have been reading directions for a casserole.

"I command you, by the power of our Heavenly Father, the Lord Jesus Christ, and the Holy Spirit, to be soothed and recover swiftly. Bake at 375° for 45 minutes or until golden brown. Amen."

"Amen," the rest of the quorum muttered in unison.

As the group of Elders—the men who had been granted positions of importance in the Mormon church—shuffled out of our living room, my parents thanked them and offered refreshments. I retreated to my room in the back of the house and gingerly sank into bed, feeling shittier than ever. I closed my eyes and waited for the Jesus injection to kick in.

Though special, these sanctifying "laying on of hands" moments were not rare. They were doled out for a number of reasons: healing, comfort, encouragement, naming children, dedicating graves, and baptisms. And—surprise!—like most things in the church, they could only be conducted and administered by men.

Eventually I did recover: the rashes faded away and drinking water no longer felt like deep-throating the devil. I was pretty sure it had less to do with the priesthood blessing and more to do with the natural lifespan of my particular communicable disease. But that admittedly sounded less cool than being restored and made whole by an invisible specter, so when I went back to school I made sure everyone knew I had been touched by God.

My family's divine journey to Mormonism began when I was two years old, in the sweltering heat of Phoenix, Arizona. A pair of nineteen-year-old boys—I mean, missionaries—knocked on our door and asked my parents that classic, religious trope of a question: "Do you have a moment to talk about our Lord and Savior, Jesus Christ?"

At the time, my mom and dad were alone in the middle of the desert looking for answers and truth. It didn't hurt that the LDS church made the standard promise of exaltation and salvation extra spicy by pressing the belief that if you make it to Grade A Heaven (there are three tiers), *you yourself* can become a God.

However, most importantly for my family, there was a built-in community. A guarantee of love and support and guidance, which is something that we were lacking in the inexorable heat of the Southwest. My parents' response to these young men's question was a resounding "YES, we have more than a moment, we have a *lifetime*." Over the next few months, we spent a lot of time together. The guys would come over to have a home-cooked meal, and in exchange would bring me presents and His blessed word. Before I knew it, we were packing up our belongings, leaving everything and everyone we knew, on our way to Mormon Mecca, aka Salt Lake City, Utah.

It was 1989 and I was too young to understand what was going on, and my parents were too hopeful (aka, naïve) to investigate further. We didn't know that Mormonism is a fairly new religion—or a business or a cult, depending on whom you ask—and one of the fastest growing in the world. The church was founded by Joseph Smith in upstate New York in 1830 and has its own tumultuous history.

Good ol' Joe and his family were known con artists (fraudulent, "treasure-seeking" snake oil salesmen) and much of the basis of their faith was actually yanked from the freemasons and other religions and texts of the time. Laughably, some of the "golden plates," an alleged sacred archaic text buried in a hill by an angel and eventually translated into the Book of Mormon, that were found were exact copies—hieroglyphic for hieroglyphic—of the Egyptian Book of the Dead, a common funerary document.

Joseph's story was that Heavenly Father *and* Jesus Christ (a twofer!) came to him in a vision as he was praying in the woods near his home, which, by the way, is an area known to be a hotbed for psilocybin mushrooms . . . just sayin'. They allegedly told him that all the existing religions of the time were fake and it was up to him to create the one true church. So he did.

Over the years the congregation grew. They were run out of town, then another town, then another town (due to more fraud, stolen money, and racketeering), and eventually ended up in the Utah Valley, where Brigham Young, Joseph Smith's successor, looked around at the harsh salt-licked terrain, isolated in all its mountainous grandeur, and declared, *"This is the place."* The name of the game for the church, like most cults, is money, control, power, and influence. Mormonism has all of this in spades, especially in Utah, where it dominates business, politics, real estate, education, and the judicial system (put a pin in that for later). The more true-blue believers there are, the more profitable they become, as members are expected to hand over 10 percent of their earnings as tithing. It's worth noting that the church does not disclose their financials, but it's been reported that they have over *$100 billion* in investment funds alone.

So how do they keep those believers under their thumb and willing to loosen their purse strings?

Remember the sense of community I mentioned earlier? The church dictated our lives in pretty much every way, especially socially. Our participation wasn't limited to three hours of service on the Sabbath. We were commanded to pray and read our scriptures every day, but we also had gatherings like Family Home Evening (studying and praying together as a unit), the creatively named Young Women and Young Men meetings, Mutual (co-ed youth group), Visiting Teaching (where the women of the Relief Society go to other members' homes to drink caffeine-free Coca-Cola and gossip about the less pious), General Conference (when the Prophet and other old white dudes ramble on and on about the perils of the modern day and how to achieve maximum purity), temple work, and seminary.

Kids who weren't practicing members of the church were at times barred from playing with the rest of us since they came from nonbelieving "bad families," and they'd often beg their parents to let them go to church on Sunday mornings or to one of the youth groups. One has to wonder: Did they give a shit about Jesus, or did they only want to be able to play Nintendo with their friends?

Throughout all of these activities we were taught to suppress our emotions, desires, and natural curiosities. In many cases we were outright brainwashed, and we were told to ignore what the "outsiders" were saying (whether that was about politics, science, education, or pop culture), because they didn't have Sky Daddy on speed dial like we—the faithful—did. The church leadership's solution to everything was to tithe, pray, and fast. They didn't ask us to swap our inquisitiveness and emotions for oppression, deceit, and mystery because they didn't have to. We willingly obeyed, following the First Presidency and Quorum of the Twelve Apostles (as they were called) off the ledge of reason, like blind lemmings clamoring for salvation.

And, of course, the church's vise grip wasn't limited to extracurriculars. The thing I get asked about the most, after how many wives my dad had, is about the magic underwear. Known colloquially as "garments"—purchased from licensed distributors, all owned by the church, duh—they're unsightly things Mormons wear under every outfit and are yet another tool used for control, especially for women (surprise, again!). Specifically designed to protect a lady's chastity by preventing her from wearing immodest clothing, the tops are cap-sleeved so one's shoulders are always covered (otherwise you might invite the devil to perch there), and the bottoms are below the knee, which is why you see such a high number of unflattering culottes and capris in the Beehive State.

We grew up hearing stories about unlucky members, houses engulfed in flames, and the only part of their bodies not ravaged by the roaring fire were those covered by the garments. Considering they're made of, like, 98 percent polyester, I think quite the opposite would happen, but the Lord works in mysterious ways, doesn't He?

Though I do believe most LDS members meant well, I was confused about *a lot* of life when I was growing up. The people around me unknowingly (and sometimes very knowingly) made me feel guilty about my existence, often in ways that were directly tied to their misguided beliefs. There is a passage in the Book of Mormon that states that the Lamanites—an ancient group of wicked peoples who were constantly battling the much more respectable and righteous Nephites—were . . . get ready for this . . . cursed with a "skin of blackness." Cursed!

As children, ones who had really only seen dark-skinned people on a screen, racism was ingrained in all our minds: People of Color = evil. And since I'm a Person of Color, that got real complicated for everyone. One day a childhood friend very earnestly asked how we could remain close confidantes when I was "dark, filthy, and loathsome." My response was that I'd pray on it and stay out of the sun that summer.

In recent years, the church has backpedaled and edited their holy texts (apparently Jesus didn't have the foresight to know how they'd be interpreted), and newer editions omit this scripture.

Much like the color of one's skin, one's sexuality just *is* and can't be controlled . . . but goddamn, does the church sure try. I was of a single-digit age when I discovered that my crushes weren't limited to boys, and more than once I caught myself gazing past them, daydreaming about one of the towheaded, blue-eyed girls instead. Though queerness hadn't been discussed with me directly, I knew that it was wrong. I could feel it in my bones. So I squashed those feelings and doubled down on being "boy crazy," which became a noted part of my personality and is hilarious (to me), because the tactic's only purpose was to deflect from the truth. Later in my life, many other traits followed a similar pattern.

So often were my childhood thoughts filled with such an overwhelming sense of shame and wickedness that I truly thought I didn't deserve to be on this planet. I never talked to anyone about these feelings and my secret stayed between me and God—whom I languished with for hours in one-sided conversations, tearfully begging Him to bring clarity to my life and to stop my disgusting, growing attraction to peoples' *personalities* (heaven forbid!).

But I wasn't fooling everyone, especially in my early teen years. I doubt it was the big man in the sky, but someone mentioned my "dandiness" to one of the Elders, and one day I found a pamphlet for Evergreen, a nonprofit dedicated to helping "overcome homosexual behavior" through conversion therapy, in my locker at middle school.

Upon my parents urging (they didn't have *all* the details but knew something was up), I eventually went to the bishop—the leader of our specific congregation, based on zip code—to discuss things with him, as we were directed to do. While we were alone, behind a closed door, this grown-ass man asked probing questions about my innermost thoughts, including what I fantasized about when I masturbated, and how often. After each reverie I trepidatiously named, he'd ask, "And?" Eventually, I got to the point where I was out of things, so I started naming foods I had eaten for dinner the night before. Mmm, mashed potatoes, white and starchy like I like my women. (I'm pretty sure I had recently seen the movie *Secretary*, which made me feel all kinds of ways.)

After he had enough content for *his* spank bank, he lambasted me for being unfaithful to our Lord, and I'm surprised the power of Christ didn't compel him to blow his load right then and there. He continued to criticize what felt like every part of my being, and I left that meeting feeling more hopeless than when I walked in. And since all of my repenting wasn't helping, I continued to become obsessed with the one thing you shouldn't obsess over as a Mormon.

Shortly after my talk with the bishop, I ventured into the majestic Uinta mountains to Oakcrest, an LDS girls summer camp. While packing, I surreptitiously printed sexy NSYNC fan fiction off an Angelfire site that featured categories specific to each member, as a group, and trysts with the Backstreet Boys. I carefully tucked it between my Bible and the Pearl of Great Price, which is basically Mormon Jesus fanfic.

Every night, after bearing our testimonies to one another around a fire, I'd regale the saucy chart-topping text to everyone in our cabin around a flashlight, voice barely above a whisper so that our barely eighteen virgin-with-big-boobs camp counselor wouldn't bust us (new fantasy acquired). Eventually my guilt got the best of me, and I threw the pages into the fire one night, the ashes of which we prayed around until it was time to go home.

After camp I decided that I was going to give the whole True Believer in Christ thing one more solid try. I stopped touching myself, started paying more attention to the sermons, and read my scriptures every day. For a while I had even myself fooled, and the next time I spoke to the bishop it was for an interview to get my temple recommend, a small card you're given that says you're permitted to go inside the most sacred spaces of worship, where many holy ceremonies are held (aka cult rituals), like eternal marriage sealings, the endowment™ (a two-part ordinance that makes you a king or queen in the afterlife), and *baptisms for the dead*. Yeah, you read that right.

Without question, baptisms for the dead were the strangest ceremony that I participated in, and that list is substantial. They are pretty much exactly what they sound like; you physically stand in and get baptized on behalf of a person who has left this mortal coil. The deceased are typically "nominated" for a baptism by their Mormon family members who don't give a shit whether it's what that person wanted or not, because they believe it's the only way they'll get to heaven. Most notably, Anne Frank had one performed for her in the Dominican Republic. I'm sure she's graciously looking down on us from Grade C heaven (she wasn't married, so she's not allowed to go to Grade A or B).

We'd wake up very early and get dressed in all white, and it was especially important that we took showers that morning and *not* the night before, so we would be pure as we entered the temple. We would pray on the car ride there, the anticipation building in our bodies. It was always a very exciting thing to do this kind of work. Capitalizing on elitism, baptisms for the dead were one of the most popular activities, done so with the knowledge that you were about to do what very few others were chaste enough to do. Note that anyone twelve and older can perform them.

Once at the temple, they'd check our IDs and temple recommends, and we'd shuffle into the most boring-ass waiting room of all time. We couldn't talk and the only reading materials were—you guessed it—scriptures. Depending on the temple, sometimes the waiting rooms doubled as viewing rooms of the baptismal font, and you could watch others get dunked into the cum of Jesus, or blood, or whatever the fuck the water is supposed to represent.

"Sister Ferrell, please come forth."

I stood up nervously; the only sound in the room was the swishing of the unflattering two-sizes-too-big ivory jumpsuit hanging off me. But as I thought about the poor lost souls I was helping to ascend to their full potential, my nerves quieted. I needed to be brave for them. A temple employee guided me through a back room, the smell of chlorine wafting through the air. I waited in line behind three other kids for my turn to slowly descend into an ornate pool, carried on the backs of twelve bronze oxen, each representing one of the twelve tribes of Israel.

Finally, it was my turn! As I entered the pool I missed the second step and clumsily caught myself on the third, splashing the elder who was already standing in waist-deep water, waiting to receive me. He smiled, unamused, and gestured for me to hurry up. He took my hand with one of his and placed his other arm behind my back. After speed-reciting the person's name and baptismal prayer, he tilted my body back and immersed me in the water. I wasn't ready (I don't know how that's possible considering the whole day was about this particular moment), and water rushed up my nose and down the back of my throat. The chlorine burned and I resurfaced with a few wet coughs.

He started over and at first I thought I had done something wrong, but this time he stated another name, and back under I went. That day I sent seven people to heaven and couldn't have been happier.

On the way home we stopped at Deseret Book (the go-to bookstore for LDS materials and gifts) and my mom proudly told me that I could pick out a new CTR (Choose the Right) ring. Adorned with a shield, it represented the righteousness one had to possess to stay the course—the Mormon equivalent of What Would Jesus Do? that left your finger a sickly green. I examined the many options closely and decided to let the Spirit choose one for me. Thankfully we had the same taste, and I slipped the purple shield surrounded by delicate flowers onto my ring finger, promising myself to God.

Despite now fully believing that the church is bullshit (by the way, this isn't limited to Mormonism—my feelings can pretty broadly be applied to any Judeo-Christian religion), I still feel like I must defend it—always with the disclaimer that I'm not, like, *defending* defending it. And maybe it's not an "it" but more of a "them"—the generally sweet but misguided members of the church who don't know any better. An unarguable truth is that there's a very strong sense of community (my parents got what they wished for), and the church and its members really do take care of those whom they see as their own.

For all of the craziness that growing up Mormon brought into my life, the church did end up teaching many lessons that would stay with me—they just weren't the ones *they* wanted to stick. I stopped believing shortly after committing myself with that cheap little silver-plated flower ring on the day I performed baptisms for the dead. I began to explore and lean into my suspicions around the church and started to take notes. I watched as my parents wrote weekly tithing checks, all while we were eating church cheese (from the "poor store") on shitty church bread.

All the confusing feelings I had of love, admiration, and lust for other girls, had I voiced them, would have been a siren song for the leaders of our ward, horny to send the weak of faith to dangerous conversion camps and group "therapy" sessions. Every Sunday, we were constantly reassured that we are all equal in the eyes of the Lord . . . with the caveat that you were a straight white man. Otherwise, you were simply one of *those people*.

I observed the ways that members were controlled and influenced by the leaders of the church, forced to do and believe all manner of things . . . all under the guise of *free will*. And it wasn't limited to the Powers That Be. Your own "brothers and sisters" became your two-faced supporters, quick to come over with a casserole and then turn around and be an asshole. Like with any successful MLM, you have someone you're trying to please, and someone who wants to please you, and the church banks on that hierarchy. It was like a MasterClass in the art of manipulation, and I was a star student with a front-row seat.

3

THE LASTING EFFECTS OF
"PAY WHAT YOU WEIGH"
RESTAURANTS

Despite the religious upbringing, and the whole thing of me being *me*, if you were to pan out and look at my life from the big picture, my tween years would seem very normal. I listened to a lot of secular music, watched too much TV, begged to go to the mall, and cycled through all the typical girl problems: Does my crush know I exist? How can I be cooler? Do I need a perm? When I was in the sixth grade my mom acquiesced and took me to a salon, where I got what can only be described as the third photo on the cover of an *Animorphs* volume, where a girl is turning into a poodle. During this same time, I also had braces (with headgear that I never wore because the thought of it was too embarrassing, even if no one saw me wearing it) and thick unfashionable glasses (a misnomer—fashionable glasses didn't exist in the '90s). If that weren't enough to be considered a hate crime, I was also short and overweight.

My hobbies included playing *Rodent's Revenge* on our clunky Compaq computer for hours on end while I stuffed my face hole with Little Debbie Swiss Rolls and washed them down with an ungodly amount of pop. I loved eating and I loved feeling full.

My favorite restaurant growing up was a family-owned Mexican joint called Garcia's. The food was unmatched, and my go-to order was a chicken chimichanga, a huge dollop of sour cream, a side of chips and salsa, beans and rice, and a Sprite (and don't give me that kid-size plastic sippy cup bullshit). Eating at Garcia's filled my family with such joy (and lard), but the act of actually dining there filled me with such anxiety that my body would seize up when we approached the building. My fists clenched so tightly my nails left imprints in my palms when we walked past "sleepy Mexican" statues (authentic!) flanking the path to the front door.

The doors were uncompromisingly heavy, and as I watched my dad exert too much effort to pull them open, I wondered if any of this was worth it at all. Inside the lobby, we found ourselves surrounded by faux bricks on the floors and the walls—the opposite of a padded room, another kind of insanity. The smell of fresh tortillas and salsa made my mouth water immediately. To the side of the hostess stand, there was a gigantic metal scale—more county fair than doctor's office—draped in fiesta flags. Hanging on the wall above it was a sign that boldly stated: KIDS = 1 LB. = 1 CENT.

"Step right up," the hostess would say, like a demented carnival barker, ready to hand out prizes to the adults and long-lasting trauma to the kids. I'd follow her orders, begrudgingly putting both feet on the scale with a nudge from my mom and my little gut sucked in tight. It's worth noting that I wasn't an obese kid—especially by today's standards—but I certainly wasn't one of the lean, long-legged, Aryan poster children who surrounded me. As soon as the needle started to move I'd pray (like, earnestly with my whole heart, because Mormon) that the hostess would be cool and jot down the total and keep it to herself instead of shouting it out for everyone to hear. (PS: fuck you, Deborah.)

To be honest, most of the time it all took place with little fanfare—you know, besides the crippling internal anguish—but not today. Today, my classmate Alanna Briggs—the same Alanna Briggs who spread that stupid, racist rhyme around the playground—stood behind us. She was with her brother and their parents and I watched as her perfectly manicured eyebrow (as thin as her waist) raised ever so slightly, taking note of my number and filing it away for later use. As we walked away I oh-so-casually said, "I should have taken my jacket off, it weighs a literal ton." It did not.

As I ate "my usual" in that sticky, vinyl booth in the corner, the aromatic food barely masking the scent of Fabuloso cleaner and wet rag, I told myself that I could stop at any time. I didn't have to eat *all* of it, but why wouldn't I when my hardworking parents spent a whole seventy cents on it? *I bet Alanna's meal was only two quarters,* I thought as I took a huge gulp of Sprite to wash down my next bite.

The '90s were an interesting time: gaunt, heroin-chic cheekbones were featured on magazine covers as the rates of obesity among non-model normies tripled. There were so many fad diets it was hard to choose only one. Your never-ending pu pu platter of options included (but were not limited to): the grapefruit diet, the Zone diet, the Mediterranean diet, the Eat More, Weigh Less diet and, of course, the Atkins diet. And if restrictive eating wasn't enough on its own, you could always add a dash of Optifast or Fen-Phen.

Unsurprisingly, the majority of people fueling the popularity of these diets and products were women. Weight loss tips and tricks were passed through whispers in the female-only classes at church, the crunch of olestra-filled chips filling the air between prayer.

It was there, in one of those classes, that I was told at a very early age that if you didn't take care of yourself you wouldn't be desirable, you wouldn't attract a husband, you wouldn't get married, and subsequently you wouldn't be eligible to go to top-tier heaven. From that moment forward, my weight was what stood between me and my eternal salvation. No pressure.

The world has always told women how they should look, no news flash there, but it's astounding how much of it is thrown at you as a child. Little girls are told, pretty much from the beginning, to be uncomfortable with their bodies during every stage of adolescence and puberty. And then, if you make it out of that alive, your consolation prize is a new fresh hell of cyclical shame.

For as much as we girls were told how to behave, we didn't really discuss how we felt, and since my interests were much more aligned with those of the boys I hung out with, there was only one girl I was close with whom I felt I could actually talk to: my favorite cousin, Taylour. For much of my childhood my mom and aunt were on good terms, so I grew up spending a lot of time with their family. Taylour and I were born the same year and liked a lot of the same things (Lisa Frank notebooks, our growing pog collections, slinking around the house pretending to be cats), but physically we could not have been further apart. Where I was short and squat, she was tall and thin. Where my skin was the color of a toasted marshmallow, she was the color of a . . . regular marshmallow.

Tay could eat whatever she wanted and not gain a single ounce. I couldn't understand how we had the same meals, and the same relatively sedentary lives, but were so different: a fact she reminded me of regularly. Not in a mean way, just perfunctory. Even though I'd never been shown anything besides acceptance from my extended family, I never felt that I belonged, not completely. How could I be when we were so different? When I would lament to Taylour, her response was usually some version of, "Well what else are you going to do? Get a new-new family?" She had me there.

One morning, after I had stared at my naked body for a few minutes (I liked to pretend I had a monster living in my torso, with nipples for eyes and a belly button for a mouth, who liked to share with me how his face shouldn't be so plump), I groaned in frustration, got dressed, and housed a massive bowl of Frosted Flakes. My mom came into the kitchen and handed me a permission slip with her wet signature at the bottom. I needed her approval, for today was the day that I would learn about becoming a woman. Today was the day we entered (and exited) the two-hour state-run maturation program.

My class was abuzz with frenetic nervous energy (except for the one Jehovah's Witness who got to get out of it—ugh, why hadn't my parents picked that religion?) as we shuffled into the gym and were separated by gender, the girls on one side of the bleachers and the boys on the other. On paper, this is something I should have been more than excited about. I was, after all, a horny little kid who had memorized the dictionary definitions for "intercourse" and "genitalia." But I also knew that the person I became when I'd sneak down into the basement to flip through old issues of *National Geographic* looking for boobs was a sinner. I reminded myself to be careful today and play dumb, to pretend to know less than I did.

Miss Harper, our elderly school nurse (in reality, she was probably thirty-five), in her denim teacher's jumper covered in handprints made of puffy paint that made her look like she'd slaughtered a family of Michelin Men in cold blood, shuffled in front of the girls' side.

"Girls. Girls! Pay attention!" The room eventually quieted as we eyed each other cautiously.

"Today we will cover many important topics like puberty, menstruation, human reproduction, and proper hygiene," she read from a piece of paper, which she then dropped. She strained to retrieve it, her own body's curves and folds getting in the way.

"Why would we want to learn about becoming a woman from a pig?" Kaidence Hatch whispered sharply.

We all snickered and started to chat among ourselves.

"GIRLS!" Miss Harper, exasperated, tried to gain control of the situation.

A boy from the other side yelled in a high pitch, "All we're learning about women is that they won't stop talking!"

Laughter erupted from the foreskin forum. Miss Harper frowned as she tried to tell us a personal story about blood rushing out of her vag, as blood rushed to her face. Our morbid curiosity took hold and we started to pay closer attention to the lesson. We looked through confusing anatomical diagrams while Miss Harper discussed the changes that our bodies would be making. There was a strong emphasis on eating properly and exercising regularly and the now-outdated food pyramid was featured heavily. Calorie intake tracking and food journaling were suggested. We were also given tips on how to "stay clean," both physically and spiritually. This was beyond abstinence-based curriculum, this was "come inside me, Jesus" territory. We never covered how babies were actually made, and at the end of the day the general consensus was that being a woman was a huge fucking pain in the dick.

As Miss Harper concluded the lesson, she thanked us for letting her be a part of our journey and told us to grab a few donuts on the way out. I grabbed three but only logged the calories for two.

The weeks after the maturation program were filled with taunts and jeers, mostly directed at the "Period Posse" as we came to be known by the monsters disguised as pubescent boys. Oh, if only we knew about their nocturnal emissions and random boners brought on by looking at the deli meat in the grocery store or going over a speed bump too fast. But all of that was hidden from us: we never focused on the male anatomy, because we didn't need to. We would learn all we needed to know on our wedding nights.

All of this would have died down a lot earlier if not for one day at PE. While we were out on the field, someone found a used tampon, exposed and bare, free of any wrappers or toilet paper. It likely came from a girl who was so terrified and embarrassed by her own body that she found running out to the middle of the lawn and fishing the thing out like a grizzly bear hunting for trout (one paw? two paws?) to be a better alternative than being seen in the public bathroom with it.

Flying through the air, string waving in the wind, the coochie Q-Tip was flung around on the end of a stick, each little dumbass trying to hit the others. Poor Ashley Koehler got caught in the crossfire and the unsanitary sanitary projectile hit her squarely in her undeveloped chest. We all squealed and laughed in disgust when she shrieked and burst into tears and raced back toward the school.

As we ran around the portables (what we called the glorified double-wide trailers behind the school, retrofitted to be the finest atmosphere for education) and giggled in relief that the tampon hadn't hit any of us, I suddenly felt a sharp tug and was pulled back a couple of steps. My head whipped around and I saw my friend Brandon Moon dart away, hand recoiled as the THWACK of my bra strap contacted my skin.

One thing I haven't mentioned is that, unlike Ashley Koehler, I had started puberty fairly young. Which meant I had boobs well before a lot of my classmates—and not what people typically think of when they think of Asian boobs. No, I had big *American* boobs, thanks to a diet of growth hormones and excess, to which I was very committed. Obviously, this did not go unnoticed, and Miss Harper and her lessons had only made matters worse.

"Ew, Kari's *maturing*! I wonder if she's going to start bleeding out of her butt next!" That fucking Andy Swanson, the bane of my existence. I'd learn decades later that Andy came out of the closet as a young adult and I wonder how much of his life felt the same as mine at the time: alone, trapped, confused.

I was beginning to notice that my body was attracting attention in ways it hadn't before. Though it made me uncomfortable, I sometimes enjoyed the sustained stares of the male gaze. The feeling was, hey, if my body—the thing that had made me stand out my entire life in a bad way—was all of a sudden different in a *desirable* way, I was all in.

It didn't take long for me to realize that I could utilize all of this *gestures wildly around body* to my advantage. I don't mean that I was doling out blow jobs in the Discovery Zone parking lot for miniature erasers (that would be in my teenage years, and it was a Home Depot). It would take time to level up. It was small-time stuff at first, like getting out of trouble when I got caught roaming the halls by a monitor (he was a year older, *a sixth grader*). I casually walked close enough to him so he could smell my Love Spell body spray, stuck out my completely covered chest, and turned on the charm. I got away scot-free and gained some skill points.

When we live in a society where young girls are forced to grow up so early, it only makes sense that we'd learn to make the best of it. Call it a learning curve, or maybe a survival tactic. The responsibility for boys' behavior, and the emotional labor required to deal with it, rested solely on us girls. We couldn't wear shorts or tank tops because they would cause distractions in the classroom. Boys could wear whatever they wanted while never being taught respect or consent, setting them up for a lifetime of objectifying women and perceiving them as lacking, all due to a little shoulder exposure.

And it's not like I was thinking so "progressively" at the time (women not being the cause of everyone's woes? Whoa!). Most of my friends were boys. I connected with them more and I liked that they spoke their mind, never pussyfooting around things. Plus, they liked video games, skateboarding, Limp Bizkit, and talking about hot girls just as much as I did (wait, what was that I said earlier about objectifying women?). And in a way these boys ultimately helped me discover my queerness, though I never would have told them that, even *if* I could have articulated it.

So the day that Brandon Moon snapped my bra strap behind the portables, I was annoyed but not outraged. I had a feeling I should be upset, but I didn't really understand why. After all, the guys were always fucking with each other: tapping balls, wet fingers shoved down dirty ears, the usual shit. If anything, part of me was honored in a way that I had been let in, that I was worthy of their attention. But still, they had to know I was unfuckwithable.

Young little Kari had the confidence to walk up to Mrs. Cottrell, the most feared teacher of them all, to let her know what had happened. Naive little Kari had the confidence to think that she would end up on top in this situation, and maybe even revered in some way—a bastion for the right to mature in a safe environment. Had I known that Mrs. Cottrell was not only a bitch, but also an antifeminist, I may have reconsidered my options. But by the time she had ended recess early and called everyone back into the classroom it was too late. Brandon and I were asked to stand.

"Brandon, can you tell the class what you did?"

"Uh . . ." Brandon paused.

"Tell everyone what you did with Kari's bra." She pointed in my direction.

My face was on fire, but I stood my ground, looking Brandon in the eye, daring him to speak.

"Ipulledthestrapbacksoitwouldhithither," he said quickly. Our classmates laughed.

"And, why did you do that? Did you want to hurt her?"

"No! No, I thought it was funny. She was standing in front of me and it was right there so I just did it."

"Are you sorry?"

Brandon nodded quickly, he wanted to get back to recess.

"Good. So what have we learned, class? We don't touch other peoples' property. And if you don't want your property touched, you need to put it away."

Not once was I asked how I felt or given a chance to speak, nor was I directly apologized to. I was made to stand there like a sounding board and told to hide my bra better. I left class that day feeling demoralized and vulnerable, while earlier I had felt like I had so much strength (unfuckwithable—ha!). The only lesson I learned that day is that the adults in charge aren't there to save you. You've got to do it all yourself.

Not too long after that incident, I had my annual visit with my pediatrician. I wanted to show him how much of an adult I'd become in the last year, seeking the approval I'd been looking for (and continue to look for) my whole life, which meant sticking my chest out so severely that he thought there might be something wrong with my spine. My mom had to tell him that, no, nothing is wrong with her, she's just a baby slut.

I remember stepping on the scale—my body clenched up, all shoulders up to my ears—experiencing the kind of PTSD that only comes with a side of rice and beans.

"Ah, seventy-four pounds. Eight pounds more than your last

visit. Let's see . . . okay that's mostly within the accepted range for your age . . . but not so much for your height," the doctor stated casually, as if he weren't sending my fragile little girl psyche in front of the firing squad.

"What . . . what should the number be?" I asked.

I was scared to know the answer, but it was the adult thing to want to know. It would make the mental math I had started to do at every meal easier. It wasn't only calories in versus calories out—it was calories of the last week's meals versus the current week, how the difference compared to the month before, divided by the weeks I had already failed, and so on. The common denominator was always my lack of self-control, and damn, I wish I had known about Excel.

"About sixty-five pounds, but don't worry. You'll probably even out over the next year or two."

Excuse me? Over the next year *or two*? Dr. Watkins seemed so nice and mild-mannered with his Ned Flanders mustache and the way he'd warm his hands up before examining you, but what he was saying painted him in a new light.

He continued, "What do you eat in a day?"

"For breakfast I eat my feelings," I quipped, cheekily reciting a phrase I saw on a novelty tee at the mall (the original meme).

Dr. Watkins frowned. My mom looked embarrassed.

"Um," I continued, "you know, the regular stuff: Frosted Flakes, pizza, taquitos—I really love taquitos—chicken-fried steak at school on Wednesdays, breadsticks, choco—"

"You're leaving out all the fruits and vegetables. How many of those do you have a day?"

I thought about the sad, soft carrots drowning in their own juice, cordoned off from the rest of the food on my lunch tray.

"Um, I like kiwis and strawberries, and orange juice."

"Great, that's what I like to hear—"

I interrupted, "Especially with a scoop of ice cream! Have you ever had an Orange Julius, Dr. Watkins?"

"Kari, what you eat is important and your physical appearance reflects the quality and kinds of food you put inside you."

Wait, was he telling me that I looked like Wednesday chicken-fried steak? All droopy and gelatinous? I started to feel a buzzing in my head. This had been happening frequently, my thoughts swirling around me like cash in one of those money grab machines on TV. I struggled to catch them and put them in order. There were so many I couldn't make sense of anything; the frustration grew and I held back a guttural scream.

Clearly this man had it out for me. Nearly a decade of excellent care down the drain. He didn't give a shit about me; he wasn't concerned for my welfare. He only wanted to collect the insurance money and go home to his massive mansion on top of Eagle Mountain. And clearly I didn't know much about small-town doctor salaries and should have been tipped off when we saw him get into his clunky Ford Escort after one of our late-afternoon appointments. In any case, he was misinformed and wrong.

Dr. Watkins asked me to go and sit in the waiting room while he talked to my mom for a couple of minutes. I gave him a cold look so he knew I was disappointed in him and ran toward the Game Boy mounted on the wall, ready to elbow any other kid that got between me and Kirby (my favorite character, a small, stubby pink sphere that went through life inhaling objects indiscriminately and . . . oh . . . *damn*).

On the way home I asked if we could stop at McDonald's. Mom gave me a look and explained that Dr. Watkins had said that I need to rein it in a bit.

I quickly launched into my rebuttal and explained to her that I needed to collect as many unique Beanie Babies Happy Meal toys as possible, as it was how I planned to put myself through college. I must have been convincing, because the next thing I knew we were pulling up to those beautiful Golden Arches. I stuffed my mouth full of deliciously crisp fries while simultaneously tearing at the box to get to my prize (awarded to me for being number-one eater). Triumphantly, I raised the small stuffed animal up, waving it around excitedly. As I freed it from its plastic prison, I yelped with excitement. I was the proud owner of the elusive Pinky the Flamingo, the missing piece of my collection!

See? I thought to myself. I *needed* to eat at McDonald's today, otherwise I would have missed my chance to get Pinky. I smiled knowingly as I scarfed down my cheeseburger before we even left the parking lot. This wasn't the only time this kind of fucked-up, cyclical logic came into play in my life, and it would soon extend well beyond food.

By and large my family didn't try to curb or adjust my eating habits. There was a brief period of time where we were getting nonfat stuff, but that didn't last long because my dad swore he could taste the difference, while my mom swore he couldn't. Our dinners were hawked to us on TV by a giant, anthropomorphic glove with a big red nose, gleefully riding around San Francisco in a cable car, content and carefree because he didn't have to worry about coronary heart disease. Around the dinner table (or around the TV trays, as it was becoming more frequent for us to eat meals looking not at one another but at a different family, *The Simpsons*) one night, my parents asked what I ate for lunch.

For the first time in my life, I lied.

I lied about fruits and vegetables, I lied about only having one slice of pizza. I lied about how many candy bars I had.

It was shocking how easily they accepted my answers. Did they believe me, or did they simply not want to deal with me? I think it was more so the former; I had never given them a reason to distrust me before. Whatever the case, I started to answer their other questions with lies, too.

"How was school?" Lie.

"Did you do your homework?" Lie.

"Have you read your scriptures?" Lie.

I told myself that I was doing them a favor, keeping them at ease, protecting them from knowing what was really going on. They didn't need to know that school was a miserable hellscape, that I didn't do my homework because I was doing other kids' assignments for them (and always aced my tests regardless), that reading the Bible only made me feel worse about pretty much every single part of myself.

Though this was the first time I had been intentionally dishonest, deception was always the name of my game: bending and contorting myself to fit in, to be one of the guys, to be a pious and dutiful daughter, to be white. It came naturally and easily, and eventually all of the lies became my truth.

4

I MEANT TO DO THAT

My heart was racing and my brain couldn't keep up. I started to panic.

"Miss, did you hear me? I need to see your receipt," the near-eighty-year-old Crypt Keeper Walmart greeter said at a decibel I struggled to hear over the pounding in my head.

I pulled out a receipt that was about four inches too short to account for all of the items in my cart that I had not-so-slyly tried to rush past a local AARP member. I glanced at the name tag covered in holographic butterfly stickers: Edna.

"I have the receipt right here, Edna. And ooo boy, isn't it crazy how much things cost these days?" I asked while channeling my inner David Blaine, waving the thin paper in the air, hoping to distract from what was happening right in front of her nose.

Edna looked at me questioningly, scrutinizing my face for any signs of betrayal.

"You talk English really good."

"Well, I did—wait, what?"

"My great-granddaughter keeps going over to Japan and I don't know how she does it!"

"Oh, uh, well she must be very smart! And Japan is so beautiful . . . especially at this time of year," I said with fake enthusiasm. "They're coming up on another festival . . . and . . ." I trailed off, noticing my friends Sam and Chris by the exit. Sam's eyes were wide as she held up three fingers, tapped her invisible watch with urgency, and hustled toward the exit. I tried to get out of *any* conversation about Asia before it got too personal, and this was no exception.

"Sorry, Edna, I'm in a bit of a rush."

"Have a great day, dear," she said, giving a little wave.

I walked briskly out of the store and a wave of relief washed over me. I did it. Not only had I gotten away, I had also won, I was sure of it.

"Kari, I thought you were a goner for sure!" Sam yelled as I approached her beat-up Honda Accord. Dented on all sides, it looked more like a twenty-sided die on wheels than it did an operational vehicle.

"Dude, what did you say to her? Did you know her? She kept you there forever," Chris said.

"Oh, you know, I charmed her with my boyish good looks," I explained, as I gave my tits a squeeze for added effect. I'd always been pretty embarrassed about my well-endowed body (see: the bra strap–snapping situation), but it wasn't until this point in my newly sixteen-year-old life that I'd learned how I could really use it to my advantage, for more than roaming the halls without a pass.

"Pop the trunk, Sam," I said.

It barely opened (the casualty of one of Sam's many accidents) and I pried the lid the rest of the way up, peered in, and whistled. Giggling, I pushed a handful of bags and loose items out of the way and hoisted the thirty-pound bag of dog food from the bottom of the cart into the car, where it landed with a satisfying thud.

"Oh yeah, I definitely won." I slammed the trunk shut with finality.

The black fuzzy dice covered in skulls that hung from Sam's rearview mirror waved wildly in the wind as we cruised down the highway, Papa Roach playing out of the one working speaker. The singer's lyrical screechy threat to take one's own life (their *last resort*, if you will) resonated with us, as we were slowly dying in suburbia and trying to combat it with our final attempt to quell our boredom: larceny.

From the back seat I watched my world pass by: small, conventional, and contained. The sky was gray and overcast, threatening to sleet as the bowl of the valley was suffocated by the inversion trapped above us. Salt Lake City is gorgeous, surrounded by beautiful snow-capped mountain ranges in all directions—if only you could see them through all the smog.

Driving away from Walmart after our carefree, victimless suburban teenage crime spree felt like the final scene of some coming-of-age B movie. Everything had worked out and we felt like winners. Well, we would have if we had been able to feel *anything*—one of Sam's windows wouldn't roll all the way up. We gagged on the eggy sulfur odor that filled the air from the city's namesake great lake.

"This car is a piece of shit! My nipples could cut glass back here," I yelled at Sam over the loud growl of the semi-truck that was passing us.

"Bitch, beggars can't be choosers! I'll get a new whip when you boost one for me! You've gotta be getting close to unlocking that level." She winked at me in the rearview mirror, and I felt my heart speed up for totally different reasons than before with Edna.

We made a right at fan-fave local burger joint, Arctic Circle (best fry sauce ever), and as we neared our destination I started to think about how exactly I was going to spend my earnings . . . or would I be benevolent and allow people to keep their loot? Only time would tell.

Sam turned into a dirt driveway, navigating her rust bucket around busted brick columns, reminiscent of landscaping jobs created drunkenly in *The Sims*. The tires spun out as she revved the engine, aiming the car between two others—a massive Honda Odyssey van on the left, and a 1986 baby-blue Toyota Corolla with random words and characters spray-painted all over it (one of the words being *ASIAN* and one of the characters a crude stick-figure Asian—you can guess how that physical distinction was made) that belonged to yours truly.

Sam's car sputtered to a stop, letting out an ear-piercing wheeze when the fan belt ceased, uh, belting . . . or fanning . . . clearly, there was a reason all of our cars were on the brink of death. We didn't know anything about them, nor did we care. Not caring was our MO, not caring was freedom, and not caring was not actually possible, which would eventually present a problem.

As I grabbed my bags out of the trunk, careful to take only what I put in, Chris lifted the dog food out and onto his shoulder.

"Whoa, whoa, whoa!" Sam shouted. "You know the rules. You have to carry your own shit across the finish line!"

"Always a stickler for the rules," I said. "Very anarcho-punk of you, *Samantha*." She hated when I used her full name.

"Less of a rule and more of a consideration to others, a bylaw. I subscribe to libertarian municipalism and you know that, *Kari-san*." Touché.

"Regardless," she continued, "if Chris walks through the door holding that, you declare yourself a team."

"I know the *bylaw*," I said while smiling at Chris. He had never won anything in his life, as was evidenced by all the bruises he tried to cover with his threadbare clearance-sale Goodwill sweaters that already had the thumb holes cut into them by the time they made it to him. He never talked about what happened at home, and though we weren't naive, we assumed if he wanted to tell us he would.

Opening the door that was already halfway off its hinges with my elbow, I set the bags down on the dilapidated floor next to a pile of trash that may have been tossed into the living room a decade ago in what we called the Round House. The Round House was an abandoned home on the outskirts of the 'burbs with a beautiful arched roof, featuring a massive red pentagram that at some point an ambitious delinquent had painted. It was supposedly haunted with paranormal activity, but I'm pretty sure Chris and his bruises, along with the rest of us misfits, were the only tortured spirits that place had seen. With my best impersonation of a nuclear family father figure, I let out a, "Honey, I'm hooooooome," and was met with a barrage of Twinkies hitting me in the face.

"Ah, the prodigal son returns!" Candy Nielson declared.

Candy was a couple grades younger than us, but we let her hang around because earlier in the year, her brother—who was a junior like the rest of us—died when he was tragically and fatally hit in the neck with a liner during baseball practice. She always made the prodigal son comment without fail, and we could all see how it healed her as much as it hurt her.

"Twinkies? Really, guys?" I questioned. "Ah, yellow on the outside, white on the inside. How *clever*."

"Listen, we have to uphold the unrealistic expectations that have been placed upon you since The Great Abandoning," James Petty quipped.

As goofy as he was good-looking, James and I became fast friends after meeting in the middle school jazz band where he was a percussionist and I was an alto sax player. James was also my current boyfriend, my second "real" one, preceded by the marching band's drum major who came on to me when I was thirteen and he was seventeen.

I scanned the ramshackle room, imagining its past grandeur, and looked at the faces of the only seven people in my life whom I truly felt like I could be myself around. The fact that I didn't quite know what "being myself" meant was what bonded us to one another; we were *all* trying on different personalities. Like an angsty Goldilocks, we were testing these out to find the one that was just right.

I jumped as Sam kicked the door open and then let it slam behind her. We—especially Sam—loved this place because we didn't have to take care of it. She lived in a house with a four-car garage and four cars to fill it, one for each person in her family (only hers was a POS, and if you couldn't guess, that was very much by choice). There was an all-season pool, hot tub, *and* tanning booth. It was beautiful and glamorous, and if you so much as scuffed a floor or wall you were destined to clean it with a toothbrush while her mother hovered over you, never satisfied. We all wished we could hang out *there* instead of in a smelly, run-down geometric hovel, but never dared to suggest it.

"Okay, kiddos! Let's see what we've got!" Sam screamed as she pulled out a composition notebook covered in novelty stickers from Hot Topic.

"First up . . . let's see . . ." She flipped through the pages. "Cheapest item."

"I got this on lock," Candy said while holding up a packet of taco seasoning. "Twenty-nine cents."

"Are there any challengers?" Sam inquired.

James interjected, "No, Candy, I am the one who *got this on lock*." He fished around in his pocket and pulled out a small screw. "Nine cents, beeotch. Suck on that."

Candy laughed and slapped James playfully with the seasoning and then handed it to him.

"Most expensive item," Sam moved on, all business.

Someone held up a DVD of *Fight Club*, Tyler Durden/The Narrator (spoiler, sorry) staring solemnly at the little kleptos before him. Chris bested it with vitamins, which Candy then bested by pulling a digital alarm clock out of her purse. We all glanced around waiting for someone else to make a move, and as I went for my back pocket, Chris pulled something out of his sock that caught the low late-afternoon light.

"A pure and genuine cubic zirconia engagement ring for only the most authentic displays of love. Forty-nine ninety-nine." Chris beamed.

Everyone clapped as Sam looked around and asked if anyone could do better. I hesitated and decided to keep the overpriced microSD card tucked away. Chris deserved this one. I was benevolent, after all.

"And finally, largest item."

Everyone turned toward me as I patted the thirty-pound bag of processed buttholes and beaks sitting next to me and smiled. No one else had a chance.

"Like I said, Kari, you're leveling up," Sam smiled.

I was practically levitating from the compliment, but the rush didn't come from stealing. My shot of dopamine came from validation.

The core group of us bad kids had met in seminary (an actual extracurricular in my public high school). During one class I asked the teacher to explain why there was no evidence of the massive battles—and subsequently millions of lives lost—detailed in the Book of Mormon. He couldn't, and I started to ditch class every morning. Naturally I ended up hanging out with the other truants, the freaks, the bad kids. They were the ones who had to be bussed in from a nearby mining town and had pictures of George W. Bush with a target drawn on his forehead in their lockers. They, too, had grown up Mormon (who hadn't?) and we connected over our malaise, our resentment, and our anger toward the establishment. Our truancy usually consisted of skateboarding in abandoned parking lots and the shit that all dumbass teens do to escape their boredom. Which, of course, included retail theft.

We had long conversations about "things the government doesn't want us to know" and the gross iniquity of the world. I wasn't *completely* ignorant, but this was the first time I was exposed to more radical ideology. The first time I was made aware of the haves and have-nots (outside of my parents telling me I had to clean my plate because of all the starving kids in Africa) and the power imbalances that defined our everyday lives. And, most importantly, it was the first time that I felt truly connected to other people on an intellectual level. They may have been "stoners" and "losers," but they were the smartest people I had ever met.

Since I felt like I was getting more of an education outside of school, I started to skip more classes, even ones that I had previously loved—mostly because they had validated me and made me feel smart, not because I actually enjoyed being in them. The only one I stuck to with any real conviction was a veterinary technician program at the local community college, because I love animals (they don't talk back). Being a vet had been my dream job for as long as I could remember, but it was slipping out of my grasp when I realized I might not even graduate high school.

The forbidden rebelliousness of playing hooky scratched an itch that I didn't realize I had, one that had begun to spread like a rash, slowly taking over my entire body. My parents were aware of my absences, thanks to automated calls from the school that I could only chalk up to clerical and technological errors for so long. They were concerned and upset, but they were also distracted, in the midst of a divorce. Karen and Terry had been married for almost two decades, and for reasons that remain totally known, one day my mom came back from a trip to Phoenix and told my dad she no longer wanted to be with him. A divorce in and of itself is pretty unremarkable, but in the Mormon church it's a big no-no, and the fact that it was initiated by a woman made it even more reprehensible.

Their separation obviously affected me and was difficult, especially when word spread at my high school, but at the same time it was a gift. It gave me something to talk about, to opine over, and it was something that made people feel bad for me. There are some who don't like pity and will do everything to avoid it, whereas I welcomed it. Pity was a way for me to take control of the situation and my emotions. Pity made me feel like I had a choice and a say in how people reacted.

A couple of months after the divorce, my mom moved back to Arizona while my brother and I stayed in Utah with my dad. As we all tried to adjust—my dad to being a single parent, my brother and I to being "abandoned" by yet another mother—my rash of rebellion started to grow and unfurl, and I found even more ways to revolt against my white-picket-fence life.

A couple of years before the divorce, when I was thirteen, I was introduced to the "straight edge" lifestyle by a friend's older brother. Straight edge (often shortened to "sXe") is a movement that is based around keeping one's body pure. At least the inside of it—being covered in tattoos is the norm. This means abstaining from drinking, drugs, and (depending on whom you ask) premarital sex. Many in the community are also staunch vegans and animal rights activists.

A trademark of sXe is hardcore music: fast, loud, and aggressive. The vocalists don't sing, they scream. And the shows (*never* referred to as concerts) are as passionate as they are brutal, with "moshing" being the main objective. Angry and frantic, straight edge kids fucking lived for them.

Though straight edge is a global ideology, with "members"

living on every continent, the movement really took off with the advent of social media. Myspace pages dedicated to abstaining provided a place for the heavily male-leaning subculture to gather, and the messaging was especially popular in Utah. The path from LDS to sXe is direct and simple, since it's rooted in giving up vices that most Mormon kids haven't tried anyway. We saw the world as corrupt (which is hard to argue) and giving into simple pleasures was for the weak. We galloped above the status quo on our steroid-free (not-so) high horses. The lifestyle felt like a safe way to rebel. But it doesn't always stay that way.

Some may say that brutality is at the core of straight edge, though most of the kids I hung out with were peaceful. Classified as a gang by the FBI, there are different factions with their own names and unique rules. And as society has taught us many times, a shared philosophy alone does not bring about unification. It wasn't rare to hear that one "crew" was feuding with another, and that so-and-so had the shit beat out of them because they were caught smoking a cigarette. Touring bands often skipped Salt Lake City and it became known colloquially as the Hate-Oh-One (a play on the area code 801) and Grudge City.

So yeah, it felt—and sometimes was—fucking dangerous and violent. And I quickly found myself in the middle of the two, and it was more dangerous and violent than I could have predicted.

"Dad, I'm headed to the show. I'll be back . . . sometime!" I yelled behind me as I walked out of the house.

I looked back and saw that he was on the phone, standing in what used to be the dining room, next to the air hockey table that had replaced our actual table after my mom moved out. Judging by the goofy smile on his face, he was talking to his then girlfriend (now wife), and he gave a little wave as I let the door close behind me.

It was a school night, but it didn't matter—the rules didn't apply to me because they didn't really exist anymore. In the months after my parents' divorce, I pretty much got to do whatever the fuck I wanted. Gone were the days where I was asked about school or my friends or my life in general. Partially because I, like a lot of teenagers, tried to converse with my parents as little as possible, and partially because my primary parent was very distracted.

I made it to the driveway to find my friend Nicole waiting in her car.

"Hey, girl. Are you ready for tonight?" she asked. "It's gonna be so sick."

"Hell yeah! Are you?"

Nicole glanced toward the back and I craned my neck around to see a baseball bat on the floor.

"I'm a pacifist, but you never know what's going to happen," she said and shrugged.

I laughed at the idea of Nicole doing anything with a baseball bat, sports-related or otherwise. We drove to DV8, an all-ages club in downtown SLC that let hordes of rowdy young adults fill the space as long as the owner's palms were greased on a regular basis. The lineup for the night consisted of mostly local bands, but the headliner was a band called Hatebreed, which should have been a good indication of how the night was going to go.

As we circled the block looking for parking, we saw our friends—surly-looking tough guys who we only knew to be menacing when they were in the mosh pit—huddled in an alleyway. None of whom were from the Round House crew (most of whom I'd ditched for this *new* new group of people). If they hadn't sworn off drugs, you might have thought they were shooting up or jerking each other off, or, if very coordinated, both at the same time.

Nicole hit the brakes and I rolled the window down.

"What are you troublemakers doing? Do I need to call the authorities?" I shouted.

They glanced up at us and one gave a halfhearted wave, and then went back to whatever it was they were looking at.

"That's weird," Nicole said.

"Yeah. Weird. That's exactly the feeling I'm starting to have about tonight," I replied.

"Well, it's a good thing we can hit a grand slam if we need to."

By the time we found a parking spot we had all but forgotten about the boys, and my body felt electric as we walked into the manufactured darkness of the basement venue. The first band was already on, and they were absolute trash. The vocalist sounded like a raccoon that got its paw stuck in the garbage disposal, but it didn't matter—they were hometown heroes, and everyone in the venue felt connected through their (white boy) rage.

The chaos of a hardcore show is something to behold. It's a

frenzied display, reminiscent of tribal gatherings and rites of passage—men proving they're men by expressing themselves the way nature intended, using their bodies to punch and kick and spin. The main adversary in this display of primal aggression was the air, but every once in a while, a fist made contact with a face and everyone held their breath, waiting to see if it was going to turn into something more intentional. I, of course, wanted a front-row seat and would stand as close to the action as possible. With my arms folded across my chest, I'd nod my head to the beat, a frown plastered on my face, trying to mimic the others.

In my mind I was tough. I was one hundred and eighty pounds and six feet tall. I was as invincible as the facade I had built around myself. I was being smug and thinking all of this to myself when a folding chair flew by my face, so close I felt the metal graze the top of my head. The music was at a decibel that masked the noise of the chair ricocheting off the concrete floor. A beefy dude wearing a TO THINE OWN SELF BE TRUE T-shirt picked it up and swung it around as he spun in circles.

As expected, the chair clipped someone and a tooth was spat out of a bloody mouth.

The phrase "all hell broke loose" doesn't seem appropriate for this scenario—hell has structure, nine circles according to Dante. What transpired was pure, unadulterated pandemonium.

It took a moment for people to realize what was going on. The band continued to play, likely unable to differentiate violent dance movements from actual violence, and I watched as the fight spread across the room like an outbreak. I could taste the testosterone (and not in a sexy way). It was thick and heavy: bottled fury that was being shaken like celebratory champagne that none of these men would dare drink.

I felt a hand on my shoulder and I spun around, fists pulled back, as if I knew how to punch anyone.

"LET'S GO!" Nicole screamed silently—the band had stopped playing but the sound of all the animals fighting was even louder.

I grabbed her arm and we navigated our way out of the mayhem. Once outside we walked to the corner, far enough to stay out of the fray, but close enough to keep tabs on what was going on. It's not like we actually wanted to leave—this was the most exciting thing that had happened to either of us in years, maybe ever.

"What the fuck?!" we yelled at each other at the same time.

My body was vibrating, adrenaline pumping as if I myself had been a part of the brawl. I jumped up and down to exert some of my manic energy as people started running out of the club. The melee had spilled out onto the street, and blows were being exchanged as cars honked and navigated around everyone.

An eighteen-year-old guy called Busted Matt (a horrible nickname given to him because of a birth defect that gave him a mangled claw in place of a left hand) walked by us, sweating and out of breath. He did a double take and then an about-face, staring at me intensely.

"YOU FUCKING BITCH!" he yelled while looking crazed and bug-eyed.

"Me?" I asked dumbly.

He came toward me, snarling. Nicole tried to step between us. He pushed her aside and got so close to me that I could see his individual pores.

"You stole from me. You fucking stole from me. YOU FUCK-ING STOLE FROM ME!"

At this point, a lot of the dudes who had been fighting with each other stopped and turned toward us. This was a much better show—it's not every day you see a man waving his disfigured limb wildly at a small Asian girl. They started walking closer to us, and pretty soon we were surrounded by spectators. No one said anything to Matt or me. They wanted to let it play out, to see what was going to happen, like Nicole and I had done with the original fight.

"I don't know what you're talking about, Matt," I replied, my voice wavering, but telling the truth.

"You came into my family's store and you stole from us. We have you on tape. You fucking cunt!" he screamed, spit flying, wetting my face.

The crowd murmured, but still no one actually said anything to us. I racked my brain, trying to remember what his parents looked like, what store they owned, what I had stolen. I was coming up blank.

Matt continued, "A few months ago you walked in and grabbed a Sidekick off the counter. It was my little sister's and she had gone to the bathroom. Ring a bell?"

Oh, shit. It was all coming back to me. That was the first time

I won the "most expensive" category. I had neglected to tell Sam, Chris, Candy, and the others from the Round House where I had taken the phone from, alluding that I swiped it from a T-Mobile store (which was nearly impossible because most of their phones were tethered and locked; ironically and unsurprisingly, my "skills" I was applauded for were also a farce). They never would have condoned stealing from an individual—we were against corporations and the establishment only.

The craziest part of all (maybe) was that I didn't even keep the fucking thing. My family didn't have T-Mobile, which the Sidekick was exclusive to. I took it simply because I wanted to be liked and accepted by my new group of friends. And it worked.

Matt looked at me, daring me to say something.

"I . . . I didn't know . . . I'm sorry, I'm so, so sorry," I stammered.

He listened to me for a few seconds as I gave lame excuses and offered to pay him back and to get his sister a replacement and then he cut me off.

"You're a fucking psycho gook bitch. Everyone here knows it," he spat, as he reached into his waistband and pulled out a 9mm gun—a Glock, to be specific.

"Matt, what the fuck? I said I'm sorry!" I started to panic.

He raised the gun toward my head, his finger near the trigger.

"Say it again."

"I'm sorry," I cried.

"Again."

"I'm sorry!"

"You fucking better be."

He lowered the gun slowly and tucked it back into his pants.

I was shaking and frightened and humiliated. I ran to Nicole's car as she followed me, dumbfounded. We slammed the doors shut and she turned the car on, then looked over at me. She started to say something, but stopped herself, and threw the car into reverse. We backed up, toward Matt and the group of people who had witnessed this all transpire, who had said and done absolutely nothing as a gun was waved in my fucking face. For a split second I thought Nicole was returning me to the angry mob. Instead, we drove straight to my house in complete silence, the only noise coming from the untouched bat rolling around in the back seat.

I watched Nicole drive away from the front porch, sighing heavily before walking into the house and quietly climbing the stairs to my bedroom. The same room that still had NSYNC posters on the wall and was filled with my favorite stuffed animals. A child's room, really. But I certainly wasn't a child anymore.

As I collapsed onto my bed and stared at the ceiling, I wondered what God had wrought when he created me.

And then, after a pause, I thought, *What a great story this will be.*

5

BABY'S FIRST GRIFT

I was at the tail end of seventeen and I was officially, unequivocally in love. Sometimes it felt like butterflies in my stomach and other times like angry wasps, which is how I knew it was real.

Charlie Connors was the victim of my affection, my third boyfriend, and my first casualty. He was, predictably, a white guy with great hair, tight biceps and a lean build, and a huge dick. A drummer in an up-and-coming non–straight edge hardcore band (one that had an actual record deal with an actual label), Charlie was anything but hard . . . a true softy, a really fucking good guy. He was brilliant, emotionally mature (or as much as a twenty-year-old can be), caring, and trusting—all of the things that make for a wonderful, easy partner. And an even easier mark.

A few weeks after the gun incident, I moved to Arizona with my mom and new stepdad, Calvin. I was following in the footsteps of my brother, who had months earlier headed south because a little boy needs his mother. And I needed Mom, too, but for different reasons. I was running away from bridges I had lit on fire with the explosive combination of shame and resentment (for everyone, for myself), and with the awareness that I was spiraling and needed to get the fuck out. I wasn't scared for my life because I had been threatened, but because I was becoming more destructive to myself than that firearm could ever be.

I tested out of high school and got a job at Banfield Pet Hospital as a veterinary assistant. By all accounts I was doing a good job at starting anew . . . but that was never really my plan. I knew that I wanted to move back to Salt Lake City—that's where my entire life was, where Charlie was—but the time had to be right and it had to be on my terms.

Charlie and I met on Myspace and we shared mutual friends who had both of us on their Top 8. Myspace was the purest form of the internet, before it became weaponized: straightforward and simple, it was many users' first foray into an online persona. People weren't as brazen as they are now, social grace still existed, and it was a young person's game, so your racist grandma's thoughts were still restricted to her nursing home.

Charlie and I soon found ourselves talking, emailing, and texting all day. I would sprint around the house, swapping one dying cordless phone for a freshly juiced one. We connected over music, movies, internet culture, and memes (before we knew what to call them). That was one of the special things about Charlie:

he was low-brow high-brow, and sexually he wasn't a prude—he was barely-not-a-virgin innocent. I, too, had only slept with one guy before, but I still felt like I had a lot I could teach him. Charlie also had a ridiculous, asinine sense of humor and could easily switch from telling a dick joke to discussing quantum mechanics at length. He had a hunger for information and a truly unique view of the world and society at large.

Our long-distance "relationship," however, was fraught from the very beginning. Though most of it was based in truth, I stirred the pot and tested the bounds of our virtual bond on a weekly basis. Charlie gave in a lot, but he also bit back. Not in a manipulative mindfuck way; his teeth were honed by overwhelming empathy and understanding that felt foreign and suffocating to me.

After a few months of playing this game, one where I was the dungeon master and he a mere player rolling dice, we set a plan in motion for me to move back home. I lied to my boss at the vet and told them that my dad was sick and requested a transfer to one of their locations in Utah. They happily obliged and sent me off with well-wishes. Calvin and my mom, though concerned for my well-being, were happy to have their space back—free from the general bad vibes of a brooding teenager.

My friend Lehi, one of the sXe kids I had stayed in contact with, flew to Arizona so that he could drive to Utah with me. Saying goodbye to the arid desert with a flip of the bird, we blasted down the highway, pushing my ancient car to its limit. Soon, the lights of downtown Salt Lake City glimmered in the distance like a beacon of hope, drawing me in like a redneck to a meth lab. I had waited for this moment for months, to return home to the hopeful man of my dreams, and was determined to make my life as much like a movie as possible. Main. Character. Energy.

Much like the plot of a blockbuster summer smash, I knew that there was a crux, a climax, a second and third act to come. I vowed, with all the determination I had, that I would get my shit together. I wouldn't fuck things up. This was my do-over. My eyes teared up as I saw the glint of the lights downtown. I was home. I had the perfect soundtrack for this particular scene: As we drove closer to the city I knew so well, The Get Up Kids played out of my shitty speakers. Matt Pryor's voice was tinny as he pleaded for someone to get him to his destination in ten minutes or less. We pulled up to Lehi's apartment just as the song ended, and I fell out of the car and onto his couch, passing out before my head hit the pillow.

The next day, I donned my cutest outfit—a shirt featuring my favorite metal band (the font twisty and barely legible) with a black bandana hanging out of the pocket of my favorite Diesel jeans—and Lehi and I drove over to the house where Charlie was living with several of his bandmates. The street was named after the state flower, Sego Lily, and was idyllic and full of residential NIMBY bliss. As we walked closer to the gorge that the community backed up against, you could hear the *dun-dun-dun-dun* of the double bass drums, the strum of the electric guitars played with ire, and the din of all the other elements of the ensemble.

I took a deep breath and texted Charlie that I was out front. After waiting impatiently for a couple of minutes, I wondered if maybe this—like so many other things in my life—was a mistake. As I debated sending him another message, we heard the door open, and I watched Charlie walk calmly (nervously?) down the short flight of stairs and across the grass toward us.

After an awkward half second, we embraced, and all of my fears melted away as he kissed my forehead. He smelled like heaven— musky, unfettered anger with notes of artificial herbal shampoo. I inhaled deeply.

"You're here!"

"I am!"

I thanked Lehi for driving me, told him he could use my car all day, and that I'd let him know when I needed to be picked up. Charlie and I walked hand in hand into the house and into his bed.

I never called Lehi to pick me up and quickly became the girlfriend who was constantly around and didn't pay rent. I loved being in this environment—it felt as creative and chaotic as the interior of my brain. There were late-night practice sessions, deep conversations about politics (that differed from the anarcho-sensibilities of my last friend group, based more in the reality of the constructs of our society, but still radically liberal), and lots of parties with lots of alcohol and lots of drugs. It was my first real exposure to duality, that you could like hardcore music but also soft melancholy indie folk rock, that you could be an atheist but still have a spiritual grounding, that you could make bad decisions but still be a good person. It felt like the "grown-up" version of the Round House crew.

Charlie's bandmates liked me enough, though that definitely could have been because I had lied to them about working for a music festival events production company, among other details about myself—namely, that I was two years older than I actually was. I was digging a hole no one told me to dig. These guys probably would have liked me as is, but I needed to show that I was also *useful*.

Not only was I the girlfriend who didn't pay rent, I was also the girlfriend who quickly became the reason that Charlie lost his focus, missed practices (often because we were fighting in the other room), and the reason he had writer's block. The guys started to call me Yoko, which is never a good thing. I knew that if I wanted to maintain a relationship with Charlie I had to back off a little bit, give him some breathing room even if I wanted to suck all of the air out of him. I desired him in a way that only an adopted young woman can love a person: desperately. I didn't know how to be in a partnership because I had never experienced a relationship that didn't feature ownership.

I turned eighteen and entered adulthood watching all my (non–straight edge) friends get ripshit wasted. By this time, Charlie and his bandmates knew I had lied about my age, but no one cared because it seemed relatively inconsequential. Anyway, it was a great party, truly. To celebrate becoming a grown-up, I promptly covered my chest with a tattoo of a gigantic phoenix rising from the ashes—a rite of passage without my parent's written consent.

My job at the vet clinic was going well, in the sense that it still existed and that I went to it (sometimes) and got a regular paycheck, so I was able to move into an apartment with one of Lehi's friends—a nice spot in a mediocre area—and pay rent to afford the life that most newly minted suburban adults lead. But I was so utterly and completely bored by general existence that I was miserable, even with friends and steady pocket money. Deeper than that, however, was the cavernous pit of my dissatisfaction. I always felt a little "off" (likely due to an at-the-time bevy of undiagnosed mental illnesses) and was never fulfilled.

About three months into my IRL relationship with Charlie, fucking and fighting were no longer enough to keep me engaged. I needed more. I *always* needed more. Adoration, excitement, control, the feeling of being useful—whatever it was, I never had enough. The emptiness surrounded me at all times, the unknowns of my life pulling me into darkness. I spiraled into the fissures of my heart, clinging onto anything and anyone I could, maybe not to save myself but to take others down with me.

What I did next doesn't make any sense, no more so now than it did then. It was acting without thinking. It was testing the limits. It was an uncontrollable urge to fuck shit up because I didn't deserve anything good, and because I wanted revenge against a capitalistic and patriarchal hellscape. Revenge against this place that I couldn't fit into, no matter how I tried.

"GOD. This is so fucking infuriating!" I screamed as I dramatically threw my phone onto the cheap IKEA couch, where it bounced off and then hit the cheap IKEA coffee table.

"What? What's going on?" Charlie asked.

I responded with a noise that can only be described as a banshee being assfucked by a baton.

"Kari, I can't help you if you don't talk to me . . . with words . . ." he said with a slight edge.

"It's the bank. There was some fraudulent activity on my account and the funds are frozen. I can't use my debit card or take money out of the ATM. HmmphhhheeEEEEEE." The banshee surfaced again.

"They can just do that? There's got to be a way you can get some cash somehow. What if you went to a branch?"

"And what? Go there every fucking day? I can't be carrying wads of cash on me like some kind of *hooker*. Is that what you think of me?" I asked, as if his idea was completely senseless. "But . . . there is something that might work," I continued.

Charlie looked at me, committed but trepidatious (a good representation of our entire relationship).

"Well, they didn't say anything about checks," I tested.

"Okay, so that takes care of, like, the grocery store, but so many places have stopped taking checks recently."

I contorted my face into something a bit more hopeless. "I wonder . . ." I started, my eyes closed in thought, "I wonder if I could write one to you and then you could cash it at your bank." *Eyes open now,* I thought. *Stare straight into his.* "I don't know, though. This is my problem, not yours."

"Well, it's worth a shot, don't you think?" My knight in shining armor.

"Really?" I asked.

"Fuck Wells Fargo," he responded.

"Thank you, babe," I said as I started to rub his cock through his pants. After all, good boys deserve good rewards.

We fucked all night, loudly and earnestly. I let him do things that I had never willingly let people do before, and I made sure that he knew that. Relationships are built on trust, after all.

As we laid on the floor, sweaty and exasperated, I looked over at him.

"What would I do without you?" I asked. And I meant it. I couldn't imagine life without him, without his kindness and empathy, without his eagerness to please me.

All of this probably makes it sound like I was in a lair, hair sticking out in all directions, Post-it notes and diagrams everywhere, planning . . . plotting a long life of scams. But that wasn't the case at all. I had no intent to scam Charlie—I truly thought we were going to have a fruitful and loving relationship, maybe a wedding, definitely not a baby. It all sort of happened. I was a natural disaster sitting dormant, waiting for the tectonic plates to shift and expose my faults, shaking the earth with my anger.

In other words: I was a miserable piece of shit. And unfortunately, Charlie found himself on the receiving end of my chaos.

The next day we walked over to America First Credit Union (for the people!), hand in hand, united against the evil that is Big

Capitalism. Burning a hole in Charlie's front pocket was a check I had written him earlier that morning for $500. We waited in line, chatting idly about *Heroes of Might and Magic* (our favorite RPG) and the most recent episode of our newest obsession, *The Colbert Report*.

"Did you know that his name is actually pronounced Col-bert, like Bert and Ernie?" Charlie asked.

"Non, non, non, eet eez from Frahnce! Zee T eez silent, oui oui, you complete *idioteque*."

Charlie laughed. "Okay sure, whatever you say."

"Next in line!" we heard from the front desk.

Finally, it was our turn. I walked up to the teller with Charlie, preparing myself for an interrogation.

"Good afternoon, sir. What can I help you with today?" she asked.

"I need to cash this check." Charlie handed it over to her.

"Happy to help," she replied, actually sounding happy. "And what bills do you want? Twenties?"

"Sure, whatever works," Charlie responded, flashing me a smile.

As she slid the bills into an envelope she said, "It's been my pleasure to serve you this afternoon."

I thanked her as I stood next to my partner, who had unwittingly become my partner in crime.

What I hadn't told anyone was that my bank account didn't have any money in it. In fact, I didn't even have a checking account anymore. Wells Fargo had closed it due to a zero-dollar balance months ago. It took almost a whole week for the $500 check to bounce.

"Hey babe, did you see my text?" I heard Charlie's voice on the phone, sounding stressed. My stomach dropped.

"Uh, no. What's up?" I tried to keep my voice from betraying me.

"Jesus, it took me so long to type that, too," he responded, frustrated by the now archaic multi-type T9 text entry system.

I laughed. He didn't.

"Anyway," he continued, "your check bounced. I called the credit union and they're saying that there are no funds in your account. Can you call Wells Fargo and figure out what's going on?"

Phew! He still didn't know that this was all my doing—I could still blame the bank.

"What? This is fucking crazy! I'll call them right now."

We hung up and I started pacing. Remember when I said I hadn't planned any of this? I hadn't even considered this eventuality—though I had to have known it was coming, didn't I? I had to get myself out of this situation. Charlie couldn't break up with me. What was the angle here? *Think, think, think, and figure it the fuck out, bitch.*

I walked into the Wells Fargo branch (yep, my grand plan was to *physically go to the bank*) across from my apartment and asked to speak to a manager. My leg shook intensely as I sat waiting, threading together a loose script of what I was going to say.

"Thanks for waiting, I'm Lynn," the manager said when it was finally my turn. "What can I help you with today?"

"Hi, Lynn. Nice to meet you," I said in my best talking-to-adults voice. "I'm having a little problem . . ."

An hour later, Lynn was on the phone with Charlie, reassuring him that the bank would figure this issue out over the next few days. I had convinced her that I was wronged by her employers through practiced confusion and measured frustration. I made her feel useful and valued, and thanked her profusely (I *was* truly grateful) and by the end, she believed me.

"Yes, sir," Lynn said on the phone. "Give us some time, but we'll get to the bottom of this." She passed the phone back to me. Relief flooded over me. I had bought myself some time.

"Babe, isn't Lynn the best?" I flashed her a quick, meaningful smile. "I'll see you later tonight. Love you."

Over the next couple of weeks, I operated a money-laundering laundromat—it was wash, rinse, repeat. I stole thousands of dollars from Charlie, and after realizing how easy it was (both to do and get out of), I also began to swindle other friends and acquaintances using the same ruse. My victims were good people who simply wanted to help a pal, and I was still convinced that what I was doing wasn't wrong, because I fully intended to have the money to pay them back once the checks bounced (and in some cases I did).

The stolen cash was then stuffed into a cereal box on top of the fridge. When I needed some, I'd take a wad out and it would be covered in sugar crystals. The money typically went to buying gifts (for myself, for Charlie, for friends, for family) and taking people out for suburban feasts at The Old Spaghetti Factory ("get anything you want, it's on me"). I didn't steal money for drugs, I stole money in hopes that people wouldn't forget me.

Charlie tried to leave me several times (because of the money, because I was psychotic, etc., etc., etc.) and I simply would not allow him to. Sex, blackmail, and collusion were weapons I frequently pulled out of the arsenal, entrapping him like an animal backed into a corner, all wild-eyed and baring filed fangs. Eventually he couldn't handle it any longer and broke things off for good. It was the first time he really stood up to me, and in a weird, fucked-up way I was proud of him.

Despite my actions, I truly did love the guy. Or at least I thought I did. In retrospect, perhaps I was in love with how powerful I felt when I was with him, using his trust and faith as the basis for my deceit. But at the time, my heartbreak felt real, in a world stacking up with lies.

BAM. BAM. BAM.

I startled awake from a deep nap that I didn't remember lying down to take. I hadn't left my apartment in days after Charlie left me.

BAM. BAM. BAM.

The blood drained from my face and I felt my body go cold. *This is it*, I thought. *They've come to take me away.*

I opened the door hesitantly and saw two officers standing on my doorstep.

"Kari Ferrell?"

"Yes. What's this about?"

"We have a warrant for your arrest. Come with us."

As I sat in the back seat of the cop car, my brain's synapses worked overtime while my body was forced, quite literally, to be still. The seat belt had started to move from my chest up toward my neck (the real-life metaphor of being slowly strangled was a bit much; like, *okay, universe, I get it*), but I was unable to adjust it because my hands were cuffed behind my back. A very uncomfortable way to ride through town, nothing like the days of cruising around in the back of Sam's shitty Honda. *This is not good for my bum shoulder*, I thought. And then, *This is not good for my life.*

We pulled up to the Salt Lake Adult Detention Center and I peered out the window. I must have driven past this building thousands of times and never paid it any mind. Now it appeared it was going to become my whole world.

I had known a couple of people who had been arrested before, but for nothing more than pissing on the street or being a public nuisance (which in Utah was a very easy thing to be deemed). They were typically held for a few hours in the drunk tank, never officially "booked," and then released with a fine to pay, maybe some community service hours to serve.

I started to say a little prayer out of habit, asking Jesus to help a girl out, wouldya, promising that I'd dedicate my life to one of service and yadda, yadda, yadda. Shaking my head, I stopped short without an *amen*, remembering that you can't scam a scammer.

The officers escorted me into the building, one in front of me and one to the side holding on to the crook of my arm. They chatted about an arrest they had made the night before, and how one of them had thought he was going to have to pull his gun out, all while tugging at my elbow to guide me left or right.

"Officers, thanks for making my time with you so pleasant," I said. "I'll be sure to write a letter of recommendation to my compatriots so they can request you for their next arrest."

They laughed and rolled their eyes, and I felt the vise grip around my elbow loosen a bit.

We shuffled through a series of heavy metal doors that opened up by an invisible force with a loud buzz for my grand entrance. The room I was led to reminded me of a community pool, tile everywhere (easier to spray the blood, vomit, and other bodily fluids off at the end of the night), with bars on the walls like a ballet studio, but made of steel instead of wood. My hands were unceremoniously unlocked from one another—one wrist untethered while the other was locked to the bar.

I did a little plié as the officers told me that someone would eventually attend to me, and then walked away. I shocked myself with the realization that terror and panic were not enough to stop me from hamming it up and putting on a show. Over the next couple of hours, the room filled with degenerates of all types: some were quiet and meek, others were tripping balls (seemingly already imprisoned in their own minds), and others were loud and aggressive. I tried to keep my head down and not engage, but they kept heckling and asked how a nice girl like me ended up in a place like this. If only I knew, toothless old man, if only I knew.

"Ferrell, Kari," an officer I hadn't seen before boomed.

I looked up and was surprised to see a pale, waifish woman with box–bleach blond hair and a frown across her very plain face. I raised my one non-shackled hand, and she huffed over to me.

"I always make a bet with myself when I see the names come up on the intake list that I'll be able to pick 'em before I see 'em, but you, *Miss Ferrell*, threw me for a loop," she said drolly. "Congratulations."

"Oh yeah," I replied, "I guess maybe I look more like a Ping or a Pong?"

Her scowl turned up at the corners ever so slightly. She let out one perfunctory snort, and said, "That's about right," as she led me to where a photographer stood, ready to snap my first mug shot.

The flash of the bulb was bright, and when I closed my eyes I could still see the bursts of orange imprinted on my eyelids. I was caught off guard and my mom's voice in my head chastised me for not "smiling with teeth." For many reasons, this was a photo that I hoped she'd never see.

Officer Oaks (the scowler) and I then moved to the next station, where each one of my fingerprints was taken multiple times. My hands were sweaty and the digital reader was having problems. Oaks was getting frustrated.

"If *this* is making you nervous, it's only going to get worse," she remarked.

I glanced anxiously at the puddle of perspiration on the little tray as it was wiped away and I was told to do it again.

I looked around the room, trying to find something to focus on so I wouldn't freak the fuck out. Scanning . . . scanning . . . like the Terminator looking for a match on an acquired target, but way less badass. Notably, there were no clocks or windows, like how casinos are designed so that people can't mark how long they've been there, and time is a thing that simply happens, so you keep feeding your money into the machine, smashing the buttons, and crossing your fingers for hours on end. It was disorienting. I didn't know whether it was day or night, light or dark. The difference being, of course, that this time I was gambling with my freedom.

"Ferrell, as you know, we have confiscated your government-issued ID—a driver's license, I believe, and we will return it to you when you depart, whenever that may be. Until that time, here is your new government-issued ID."

I took the card from Officer Oaks and thanked her. For what? Who knows. I was already so good at speaking the language of the oppressed. I examined the ID and saw my face staring back at me, looking surprisingly calm and collected. It was a good hair day and the locks framing my face were giving off angelic cool-girl vibes. Was this . . . was this the best photo of me ever taken? I wondered if I'd be able to buy a higher-res print (I could and did!), because even in arresting times my vanity couldn't be silenced.

"Follow me," Oaks said, tone shifting with more of an edge.

We walked down a long hallway, my hands behind my back once again, past many rooms with closed doors. The walls were painted institutional yellow. You know the shade: like egg yolk gone bad, typically relegated to DMVs, hospitals, and the shittiest of daycares. We stopped abruptly at a small room that held a small cell. It wasn't an old-timey cell with bars; it was more like a gas chamber. It was fully enclosed with a solid metal door that went from wall to wall and had a small slit for a window, obscured from the outside by a sliding panel.

"Step inside and turn around," Oaks ordered. "Have you ever been strip-searched?"

So *this* is what she meant when she had said it was only going to get worse.

"What? No! Is that what's about to happen? You're not even going to buy me dinner first?" I asked, trying to ease my own anxiety with a bad dad joke.

"No, I'm asking for my health," she shot back as she removed the handcuffs. "I love looking at criminals' booty holes day in and day out. I'm living the dream."

Uhhhh, what was that? I clenched up tight.

"Turn toward me."

I dutifully obeyed.

"When I step out, take off your clothes and place them in this container," she instructed while handing me a dingy, plastic, gray TSA-style bin. "I'll be back in a couple of minutes."

Presumably I was stripping so that she could inspect my naked, exposed body, so why was she acting like I was about to get a massage? Why leave at all? Was she compassionately allowing me to maintain some dignity?

Far more than a couple of minutes later, Officer Oaks returned.

"Okay, so here's how this is going to go down."

As she was detailing the way in which she was going to inspect my goose bump–ridden body, using language that I can only imagine she was legally required to, I spotted a green fleck in her mouth lodged between two incisors. Officer Oaks hadn't left to give me privacy and preserve my self-respect. She had stepped out for lunch.

The pat down began and her gloved hands slid over my skin, starting at my feet (which I had to lift so she could clearly see my soles), up my hips and slim waist, brusque palms dragging under and over my breasts, up to my mouth (which I had to pull open with my fingers, moving my tongue around so she could examine every inch). When was the last time I had been touched like this by another woman? Why was I thinking about *that* at a moment like *this*?

"Turn toward the wall, bend over, spread and cough," she directed.

I hesitated.

"Don't worry. You've seen one, you've seen 'em all," she said, which I knew from experience was a lie.

I contorted my body into an upside down U, grabbed a cheek in each hand, and revealed my balloon knot to Officer Oaks. I looked at her through my legs, trying to find approval in her upside-down face. If I had to show someone my butthole, I wanted it to be the best butthole they had ever seen. I gave a fake enthusiastic cough.

"Okay, Ferrell, that's enough. And for future reference, you don't have to get that low."

She handed me a stack of clothes and stepped out of the cell. What did we have here? One pair of fire engine–red scrub-like pants and a top to match, with big block letters reading INMATE printed multiple times, ensuring the wearer would never be mistaken for a medical professional. A pair of threadbare socks on their last leg (or foot? Har har). A sad sports bra with elastic that looked like it had been stretched to its limit. One pair of well-worn panties, the color of which can only be described as dead salmon (or Rose Bisque, if you're Benjamin Moore). I brought them toward my face to give them a little sniff and was thankful to find that they had a faint smell of cheap detergent and nothing else. And finally, a pair of bright orange slip-ons that were a size too big.

After another "couple of minutes" Officer Oaks came back and I wondered what was next. She told me that because I wasn't a violent criminal (only a regular one) I'd be able to have my hands cuffed in the front. She handed me a dingy plastic cup—*were those teeth marks on the rim?*—and a cheap toothbrush.

"Let's go."

We left the cell and I trudged toward an uncertain future, through a never-ending labyrinthian concrete maze, a rat race to nowhere. Branching off the hallway were many other hallways—I anticipated turning at every one, but we pressed forward.

Jail is often described as a nightmare, but it didn't feel like one to me. It was more like how it feels right after you wake up from one. Everything was confusing, but vaguely familiar—memories of moments that didn't actually happen, disappearing like smoke in the wind. I looked down and realized at some point I had been handed a thin sheet and blanket that was being carried by hands that looked like mine but felt detached from my body.

Eventually we came to a door that opened, again thanks to some sort of omnipotent, hidden force. We walked into what I soon found out is referred to as a pod: a massive room with two floors, metal staircases on each side of the large room, ten cells on each floor. Each cell had a full plexiglass wall. Curious faces were pressed up against most of them, so many women staring out of their fishbowls at the fresh meat. Someone whistled. Another growled.

"Ferrell, you'll be in eight," Oaks said to me, and then, "Pop door eight," into her walkie-talkie. After the loud *pop* of the heavy sliding door, Oaks pointed and said, "Off you go."

I walked forward, head high, trying to exude as much confidence as someone who just had her anus inspected could possess. As I neared the cells, a disembodied voice from above called out, "Dragon lady!" followed by another shrill whistle that bounced off the walls. I entered my new micro-studio apartment furnished with a bunk bed and stood for a beat, trying to ground myself. My thoughts raced: *How long am I going to be here? Am I going to get shanked? Am I going to have to shank someone?* I shuddered at the possibility.

"Inmate, close the door!" a voice demanded over a small intercom on the wall.

Flustered, I put my things down on the bottom bunk and looked around dumbly.

"Slide it shut! You're going to get us both in trouble, you idiot," a voice from the top bunk hissed.

I pushed the heavy door shut until I felt a bit of resistance.

"Inmate, close the door *all the way!*"

"Push it until it clicks!" my new roommate said with a sigh. To this day, one of my greatest social anxieties revolves around doors (but not revolving doors, those are easy enough), and whether you push or pull or slide them.

I sat down on the thin mattress, if you could even call it that. It was more reminiscent of the kind of pad you put underneath your sleeping bag. It hissed under my weight as air escaped from who knows where, flattening and becoming even less of a mattress. I took a moment to survey my new surroundings. Obviously, it was small as shit: toilet in the corner with the tiniest sink affixed to the top, a small metal table with a stool, and the aforementioned bunk beds.

"I'm Daniela, but everyone calls me Lucky," said the unluckiest person I had met so far. "What are you in for?"

"Kari Ferrell . . . and I'm in for—" I glanced at the rap sheet the jail had printed during my intake. "Third-degree felony forgery."

"Okay, damn. I pegged you for drunk driving," Lucky said.

"Third-degree felony identity fraud," I continued reading.

Lucky's head popped over the edge of the bunk bed so that her face was only a few inches away from mine.

"Damn, okay, we got a conniving li'l bitch on our hands!"

"And three counts of issuing bad checks, all third-degree felonies." I folded the paper back up slowly, trying to sandwich my remorse and embarrassment between the creases.

"Okay, *LISTEN UP, PUTAS!*" Lucky shouted out to the pod through the glass of the cell wall, "This is Kari, *es una perra chingona*. She a dragon lady and she be breathing fire, yaheard?"

"What's she in for?" someone shout-asked.

Lucky looked at me, urging me to speak up for myself.

"Um. Hi, everyone. I'm Kari."

Silence.

"And . . . well, I wrote a few bad checks."

"Speak up, ho!"

"I STOLE A BUNCH OF MONEY," I yelled.

"She's got five felonies!" Lucky chimed.

"ALLEGEDLY!" I added.

My captive audience whistled and cheered and banged on their doors and I was, for the first time, living my truth. Saying it aloud—I stole money!—felt as oddly empowering as it was imprisoning (literally). Taking ownership was new for me, and I patted myself on the back.

As I fell asleep that night, with my rolled-up pants used as a pillow, it wasn't lost on me that my honesty had only come when I had nothing else to lose.

6

LEXICON ARTIST

Talking has always gotten me into a lot of trouble. When I was a kid the only negative feedback that my teachers—all of them—would give my parents was that, though I was a great "gifted" student, I wouldn't shut the fuck up.

Words are my forte. They're how I made people forget that I was an alien creature in a foreign land. They're how I got myself into things, and how I got myself out of things. Words have, and always will be, my *"with great power comes great blah blah blah."*

And words are how, in part, I got out of my first stint in jail as quickly as I did. On the fifth day, using half an hour of the very limited "free" time outside of our cells we were granted, I attached my ear to one of the four old-school pay phones soldered to the brick wall in the common area. I would usually reach out to my friend Mason, one of the only people who would accept my collect calls.

"Kari, what do you think I can feasibly do in this situation?" Mason sounded exasperated and worried.

"Mason, that's what I'm asking you. Can you please call George at Beehive Bail Bonds and see what our options are?"

Subtly passing the responsibility off to someone makes them feel, well, responsible and way more likely to do what you want. This was no longer my problem, it was *our* problem.

"Okay," Mason sighed. "What do I say?"

I lit up with equal measures of joy and irritation, as if this were a situation that every person had to deal with at some point in their life, so why couldn't he fucking figure it out? Mason was being unbelievably kind, but there was limited time. "Mase, call him. He said he can help. I only need someone to sign off for me. You know I know I fucked up and it will *never* happen again," I pleaded, using words that I had convinced myself I truly believed.

"You have thirty seconds remaining."

Time was literally ticking, and each moment trapped inside of this hellscape made me feel like a frog being boiled alive. I was terrified that I'd acclimate to the bubbling water and resign to my fate.

"Alright, I'll call him."

"Thank you, Mase! Thank you, thank you, thank you."

"You're such a fucking bitch."

"I know . . ."

"I love you. Don't get stabbed."

The line disconnected and I was left to wonder if he hung up or if our time had expired. I was obviously elated that he had agreed to call, and my hope was that Bail Bond George would be persuasive enough to convince Mason to do what needed to be done, aka, put up collateral and legally accept responsibility for me. No big deal.

When you're locked up, *everything* is something to agonize over. The "what ifs" consume you. I worried about the most innocuous things—When would I be able to catch up on my favorite shows? What scandalous celebrity gossip was I missing?—with the same intensity that I worried about the future prospects of my entire life, and the lives of the people I had hurt.

That night my anxiety was exacerbated as we didn't get let out of our cells for our before-9 P.M.-bedtime-romp. It could have been because the entire jail was on lockdown (which didn't happen infrequently; fights, drugs, we didn't always know the reason) or because the guards simply didn't feel like it (another thing we were left to wonder about). Regardless, I wasn't able to call Mason to grill him about what George had said, and so another day of sitting and toiling away came and went.

The next day while I was walking to the shower, carrying my raggedy-ass towel stained by the previous owners with who knows what and the jail-provided Bob Barker–branded soap (unfortunately not the spay-and-neuter-your-pets game show host BB), an officer shouted my name and told me to grab anything I wanted to take with me to the outside world. I wanted none of it and high-tailed it out of there.

The meager possessions I was holding while being booked into the jail were returned to me—a carpetbag coin purse that I had stolen from Anthropologie, my dingy driver's license, one hair tie, and my beat-up Samsung flip phone—along with a one-way bus ticket and a printout with a court date set for the following week. I walked across the street and stood by the bus stop, inhaling fresh air, never having been happier to be waiting for public transportation.

I powered my phone on and texted Mason: *TY! I owe you big time. Whatever you need.*

A few seconds later I received a response: *You DO owe me. $1,000 ASAP!!!*

The next few weeks were fairly uneventful, even if they did involve standing in front of a judge (where my case was pushed weeks into the future—fine by me!) and trying to make amends with Charlie. He wanted absolutely nothing to do with me, for good reason, and had become immune to my powers of persuasion, even when they involved the promise of barely legal beaver.

In addition to paying Mason back, though I hadn't been convicted of any crimes (yet), I still had incarceration-related fines to pay. Utah adheres to a "pay to stay" program, which is as fucked-up and hostile as it sounds. Chateau ADC (Adult Detention Center) charges inmates ten dollars a day even though the privately owned jail is making on average $150 per prisoner per day from the government (aka you, the taxpayers). If you can't pay, your ass is back in jail, so they're making money off you either way. It's a win-win for the carceral state. And since I no-showed for a few shifts at the vet clinic (because I was, y'know, detained) I had lost my job and didn't make any effort to get it back.

I pulled my trusty Bank of Boo Berry off the top of the fridge and counted the few bills I had left. $350. Not nearly enough to pay Mason back, let alone my rent. So, I did exactly what the State of Utah's Department of Corrections hoped for: I started to reoffend.

This time, however, I vowed to myself that I would stop fucking over people I knew and only go after the big guys, the ones who deserved it (therefore making my actions *honorable*, if anything): predatory check-cashing spots and financial institutions, which I don't feel very bad about to this day. In between spinning yarns and running circles around apathetic tellers who wanted me out of their face, I'd go around town depositing my own bunk checks into ATMs that allowed you to cash them immediately. Eventually the banks caught on, but I still hadn't been caught.

One night, using stolen money (was there any other kind?), I took a few friends out to the culinary marvel that is Benihana. As we sat around a communal hibachi grill, we oooh'd and aaah'd watching onion volcanoes erupt and airborne shrimp land in the front pockets of button-up shirts. We consulted our menus, trying to decide which meat we'd like to see prepared right before our very eyes, when I noticed the couple next to me glancing in my direction. The guy prodded the girl, and she leaned over toward me.

"Can I ask you a question? I was wondering what this is," she said, pointing to one of the entrees that didn't have a picture.

"Oh, uh, well . . . let's see . . ." I read the description. It seemed pretty straightforward. "Sounds like it's a noodle that's deep-fried to shit and served on a bed of lettuce."

"And is that something you would eat?"

"Sure, I guess so. But tonight I'm going for the steak," I replied, happy to have made a decision.

"But, I mean, is that something you eat at home?" I stared at her, trying to figure out what she was getting at.

"Like, at home with your family. How authentic is it? I can't eat all the things you people do—too slimy and smelly."

I felt myself grow warm, temperature rising to the point where you could fry an egg on me with a flamboyant flick of a spatula. I turned my entire body away from the couple and faced my friend, told her that I wasn't feeling well, and that I had to go. I threw a $100 bill at her and walked quickly out of the restaurant.

Outside, I realized that I hadn't driven and we were miles away from home. I felt tears and rage and embarrassment well up inside of me, both because of what that bitch had said to me and because I *also* didn't particularly like unfamiliar ethnic food and had somehow become the face of it.

My fury grew and I thought about how I wanted that couple to feel my wrath. I walked back inside Benihana, fantasizing about stringing them up by their toes and giving them little paper cuts all over their stupid fucking squishy bodies and then forcing them to eat one another with a plastic fork and knife. How's *that* for authentic cuisine? I rejoined our table, apologized to my very confused friends, and ordered my steak medium rare.

As dinner was winding down and we were getting ready to leave, I dropped my fork and knocked over a glass of water while trying to catch it. Bumbling and apologetic, I knelt down to sop up the liquid and retrieve the rogue utensil. In the midst of the commotion I quickly grabbed Miss Authentic's purse and shoved it inside the coat draped over my arm.

This time as I exited the building, I felt triumphant.

After the Benihana dinner ("it's not just a meal, it's an experience!") a more conniving and purposeful drive took hold of me. The more my identity issues were exacerbated, the more my "who cares?" attitude was in control. How could I care about what happened to me when I felt like I barely existed?

Miss Authentic turned out to be Olivia Ambrose and I was in possession of her half-used ChapStick, stained Coach wallet (which contained an expired ID, a debit card, and a Best Buy gift card), dime store romance novel, and a book of a dozen blank checks.

Since the banks had picked up on the fact that I was scamming them, all of my accounts had been permanently closed. I wasn't able to pull my old stunts, so I reverted back to my original winning game plan: fucking over people I knew. I stuck to my story about how I couldn't access my funds, but this time told my friends that my *other* friend Olivia would help me out by writing a check to *them*. If they were ever suspicious, they never listened to their gut instincts, and I'd have cash in hand the following day. It helped that very few people knew that I had recently been in jail for writing bad checks.

Running scams was like opening Pandora's trash can. Once that shit was open, there was no turning back.

BAM. BAM. BAM.

I awoke with a jolt. This felt oddly familiar.

"Kari, open the fucking door. We know you're in there!" a voice yelled. I recognized it as my friend Ethan's.

I froze and considered my options. On the one hand, I could open the door and try to talk my way out of an already-at-its-peak situation, and on the other hand, I could run and hide. As bold-faced as I could be with my lies when *I* was calling the shots, once confronted I became a sniveling little pussy bitch. I chose flight over fight (where I had literally no ground to stand on) and ran into my bathroom and locked the door.

"Kari! You owe me fifteen hundred dollars! Come out here now!" Stacey, someone who had cashed an Olivia check for me, screamed.

BAM. BAM. BAM.

My phone buzzed and I looked at the text I had received: *come out and talk to us or we're going to have to call the cops.*

Heart in my throat, hands shaking, I dialed a number and waited for someone to pick up.

"911, what's your emergency?"

"Hello," I whispered frantically, "there are people trying to break into my apartment."

"Okay, ma'am, where are you located?"

I started to give the operator my address when a flash of clarity disrupted my stupidity. Jesus fucking Christ, I was calling the cops on myself. I hung up the phone as I heard my front door click open.

"Kari, are you here?"

I heard footsteps approaching the bathroom and braced myself. The doorknob wiggled and Stacey told Ethan it was locked.

The next thing I knew Ethan, Stacey, and Marina (silent but deadly) were staring down at me, my trembling body curled up into a ball with my face against the cool tile.

"Get the fuck up, Kari," Stacey demanded. "This is pathetic."

I slowly pulled myself to a seated position and looked at their faces, a mixture of pity and anger across them.

"What is going on? Are you out of your mind?" Marina asked, finally speaking up.

"Do you really want me to answer that?" I replied, defeated.

"Oh, come on, as if *you* are the victim here. What bullshit! Where's my money?" Stacey screamed.

"Stace, come on, let's try to talk this out," Ethan said evenly.

"You have got to be kidding me. She steals thousands of dollars

from me and *I'm* the one who has to calm down?" Stacey shot dag-
gers out of her eyes. "You're a vile person and I wish I had never met
you. Pay me back in the next two days or I'm going to the police."
She stormed out and Marina followed.

Ethan looked at me sternly, his brow furrowed.

"I . . . I really don't know what's wrong with me," I muttered.

His face softened and he asked what he could do to help. I
burst into tears. After all of this—the backstabbing, the brazen
lies, the bounced checks—he still wanted to help.

"We can, I don't know, get you into rehab or something."

His kindness made me feel even more miserable and I wanted
this conversation to end. I promised that I'd look into it, would
pay Stacey back, and thanked him (and meant it).

That night, for the first time ever, I devised a plan. I couldn't
make amends with everyone, but I could do the next best thing:
disappear. I had to get the fuck out of Utah. I had to go where no
one knew me and I could truly reinvent myself. I had to go where
the madness was, so that I had a chance at feeling sane.

I knew from a young age that I wanted to live in a bigger city, a
place with real culture, with people who looked like me and where
individuality was celebrated, and hustle was not only encouraged
but required. New York—though I had never set foot in the city—
seemed to check all of the boxes and then some, starting with how
it was conveniently located thousands of miles away from every
person I knew.

Within a week I had found an apartment in Prospect Heights,

Brooklyn, through a random girl on Myspace I'd stumbled on and added because she was in Michael Cera's Top 8. She happily introduced me to a comedian friend of hers who was going on tour and needed someone to sublet his windowless room. After a bit of back-and-forth, the plan was set in motion. I was moving to New York! A new start, a new life, a new me. It had all the makings of a feel-good rom-com, if only it weren't for the whole getting out of Dodge and running from the law part of things.

My suitcase with all of my belongings was packed, and I used money I don't remember the origin of to buy a cheap ticket to freedom. Leading up to my move, I said goodbye to the handful of kind souls who had, despite everything, continued to try to help me. There were no tears. We all felt only relief. I contacted my parents for the first time in months to let them know I was headed east, and my mom said what she always did: *Make good choices.*

On the way to the airport I looked out the window at the mountains, steadfast in their enormity, scared and enthralled that this would be the last time I laid eyes on them. The world whizzed by, and my mind jumbled from the adrenaline of finally being the one to abandon something and not the other way around.

Navigating the airport and getting through security took place with little fanfare. I struggled with not telling every TSA agent that I was on my way to bigger and better things. After forty minutes of killing time in a Hudson News across from my gate, it was finally time to board. I took a deep breath and walked onto the plane, hoping that the middle seat I was assigned, sandwiched between a cranky baby and an even crankier businessman, was a good omen—like a bad storm on your wedding day.

A little after 7:00 A.M. ET (my new time zone!), we hit the tarmac at JFK, hydraulic brakes booming as the plane shuddered to a stop. My new existence hath arrived! I exited the plane with the cocky confidence of someone in her early twenties who had scorched the earth, red-eye cross-country chemtrail demons following her across the sky.

As a black car whisked me away from the bustling airport to my new home in Brooklyn, panic set in. Maybe this was a bad idea. How could I be so arrogant in my certainty that this was the right move? I was a small-town girl, after all. Could I actually survive here, much less *thrive* here?

The driver stopped short in the middle of an intersection and I gawked at the people walking by, in the way that you can only when in the back seat of a meterless cab, windows tinted to the point of opacity. I was taken by how ordinary everyone looked. My heart sank for a split second, crushed by the realization that maybe New York was like everywhere else—when an impeccably well-dressed total knockout of a woman spun around to give someone the finger, mouth moving animatedly as she yelled "Fuck you!" at an apparition I couldn't see. I was thrilled.

We neared Prospect Heights, passing groups of men shouting on the corner, pulling at their hair, and cursing the cheap plastic dice they were throwing onto a large, stained piece of cardboard. We drove by a small triangular park with a line of people parallel to the wrought iron fence. My first thought was that it was a bread line or a needle exchange (oh, liberal New York!)—but as it turned out, they were waiting to play chess on a permanently fixed board, like those in the famed Washington Square Park that I only knew through Henry James novels and Patti Smith songs.

The car pulled up to a nondescript red brick building on Bergen Street. This was it! The place that would inspire change, creativity, transformation, and reformation, and all of the other things I thought I'd experience and become by living here. As I climbed the stairs, my brain was overtaken by grand visions of friends (whom I hadn't met yet, their faces an amalgamation of all the people I had seen over the past few hours) complaining about the flights of stairs, only to find that it was all worth it once they entered my fabulously designed apartment (*framed* band posters covering the walls).

Seconds after I knocked on the door, an affable guy with bleached blond neo-punk hair appeared and welcomed me in.

"Hi! You must be Car-ee, I'm roommate number one, Jared."

"It's actually pronounced Care-ee, but I'll answer to most any-thing. Nice to meet you," I quipped with a smile, already annoyed with myself that I didn't establish *who I was* in *my* new city.

As we stood in the narrow hallway, Jared gave me a quick tour through a series of pointed fingers (Jared's bedroom, Lisa's bed-room, Richard's bedroom, one more bedroom belonging to Mike, bathroom, kitchen). My dreams of glamorous fêtes and costume parties were pushed out by visions of stepping over intoxicated strangers on the way to the cramped shared bathroom. *It's okay,* I thought. *I can work with this.*

"Aaaand here you are," Jared put his hands out like Vanna White, showcasing the stark room that was to be my sanctuary from the bustling city streets. It had absolutely no style or character, but it was (temporarily) mine.

Besides a pile of American Apparel separates in primary colors, folded like delicate pieces of spandex origami in my suitcase, one of the few possessions that moved across the country with me was my checkbook. I reached into my roller bag and quickly hooked a bright red leotard around my finger, pulling it out by the crotch, careful not to touch the ten blank pages in the process, as if they might sear my flesh.

I don't know why the fuck I packed those fucking checks.

Sure, I moved to New York because I felt like I had to if I wanted any sort of life worth living, but I also really wanted to better myself and change. Under the layers of selfishness—baked in tiers like a toxic chocolate cake—there was an intense awareness of self, and I longed for the day that I could have meaningful relationships with people that were based in truth.

What I grappled with was how to continue to be good in a world that punishes kind people. Mr. Rogers always said to "look for the helpers" in times of turmoil, but whenever I found them they'd be getting kicked in the face by a richer, more ambitious person in power. I didn't want to blame the world for the way I was. In my firsthand experience, most underdogs stayed underdogs—

the basketball team of mouth-breathing, overweight snotty kids don't win anything besides more prescriptions for inhalers. And even if they do win a game, they don't continue to win. They're top dog for a fleeting moment, and then they're right back at the bottom of the puppy pile the next season.

I knew that there was self-preservation in being kind, in being generous, in being good. But all I could consciously think about was how to survive. I was quickly learning that the *mere desire* to do something isn't always enough. Ask any addict and they'll tell you about the countless times they felt true conviction to quit and then the next second they're freebasing crack out of someone's asshole. And, ultimately, that's what I was: an addict.

For the first several weeks I lived in New York, I was on the straight and narrow. One day I was at the Brooklyn Public Library, next to Prospect Park, using their computers to check my email and shoot off résumés to companies I never planned on hearing back from. The computer next to me was being operated by a waifish man with nautical stars tattooed on his elbows and a deep V-neck tee covering his chest. He chewed on his beautiful bottom lip while staring intently into the screen. Suddenly the table screeched as he pushed it away and shot out of his chair toward the printer. I leaned over to see what he was so deeply invested in but couldn't make anything out before he came bounding back. He must have seen me side-eying his shit, because he gave me a copy from the stack in his hands without me asking. I looked at the paper, a black-and-white copy of newsprint, SHOWPAPER ISSUE 32 in big, bold letters at the top.

"They never print enough, y'know?" he said.

Of course I didn't know, but responded, "Yeah, tell me about it."

After he left I examined the paper. It was organized chaos with the smallest legible font size possible—and a lot of it. Categorized by date, spanning the upcoming two weeks, was a comprehensive list of every DIY show in the tristate area, plus horoscopes and missed connections. I clutched the photocopy to my chest and gave it a little squeeze, seeing it as the treasure map that would lead me to my new friends.

A few hours later, after a shower and an orgasm brought on by my own probing fingers (probably thinking of Library Guy's cutoff denim shorts), I was walking up to the bar at Glasslands on Kent Avenue, a *Showpaper* favorite. I ordered a Sprite with lime and requested that they put it in a cocktail glass so it looked like I was a real adult (I'd learned I was allergic to alcohol, and it's probably a good thing—I suspect I'd be a mean, belligerent drunk). Thankfully the bartender didn't charge me, and I put one of my last remaining single bills on the bar, waiting for the right moment to make sure that he saw me do it.

I surveyed the room, taking in the faces of the mostly white crowd. A wave of minority malaise passed over me but was quickly ushered out by the strum of a guitar being sound-checked. An errant smoke machine pumped cold fog onto the dance floor, my sense of purpose disappearing with the walls. Parting the smoke with my hands, I descended deeper into the darkness, traveling beyond the veil of reason, and emerged on the other side a succubus.

I walked with determination and made a beeline toward a boy I had been eyeing in a fire engine–red hoodie. He looked like Jake Gyllenhaal if he skateboarded, lean and muscular. He looked like someone who would let me use his face as a Sit 'n Spin. He also looked like someone who wouldn't have thought about me twice in high school. He was exactly my type.

His cool blue eyes pierced through the darkness, watching me as I watched him give me the once-over . . . and then he looked away. *I bet if I were blue-eyed and blond this wouldn't have happened,* I thought, and my feelings of shame were replaced with maladjusted and misguided anger.

I went back to the bar, nicked a pen from the counter, and jotted something down on a napkin. I walked toward Fake Gyllenhaal for a second time.

"I have something for you," I declared.

This was met with a raised eyebrow and a quizzical look.

I pulled the napkin out of my back pocket with such speed that it seemed conjured out of thin air. He took it from me, slightly hesitant but intrigued—the best kind of mark, because they feel like they're being brave and that endears them to you—as I did an about-face and walked around the corner, peeking to watch as he read my note. His eyes moved from left to right and then got wider. He laughed and looked around, scanning the room for my face.

Like my magic note, all of a sudden there I was, directly in his line of sight. His flirtatious stare mirrored mine and I knew he was locked in.

The next morning, I slowly crawled out of the bed, careful not to disturb him. I looked around, impressed not only by the space (skylights!) but also by the furniture. Nothing too flashy, probably stuff his mom picked out for him at West Elm, but it was cohesive and calm. This was by far the nicest apartment I had ever been in. I frowned at the thought of my own "as is" IKEA dresser, nicked and dented like me.

As I stood by the bed in my bra and no underwear (like Winnie the Pooh—how did that happen?) I stared at the exposed brick (!) and one of the framed pieces of art hanging on it. By itself—a series of lines and circles (groundbreaking)—it wasn't that impressive, but as I got closer I noticed the gold screw holding it in place. This wasn't a normal run-of-the-mill screw. Nay, this was a fancy, highfalutin screw. The kind you have to go to a specialty hardware store to find and that has specialty tools to bolt it into concrete. At this moment, I realized this guy wasn't a "fuck and duck." He was someone I should put some more time into. A special kind of screw.

This was the first time I actively made the decision to ruin someone's life (or at the very least, completely dismiss their well-being).

In Utah, all of my bad checks were written to close friends, which is horrible on many levels and not usually the way you start an "it gets worse" story because it *is* the worst. Quite simply, I truly thought that by the time the check bounced I would have the money to pay the person back. And it's because for a while that's actually how it worked out. The first few times I received the inevitable "there's been a problem" call, I'd say, *Oh wow, I'm so sorry, I don't know what happened. Things are fixed now and I'll drop off some cash later today.* Never mind that most of that cash came from running the same scam on other friends.

These thoughts swirled around me like a tornado, synapses firing at full force, as I thought about everything and nothing all at once. My brain conjured up faces that flashed in front of my eyes, friend after friend after friend whom I had fucked over. A loud snore startled me and brought my undiagnosed ADD-riddled brain back to reality. With a shake of my head, I looked back at the boy in the bed.

Yeah, I was gonna steal some money from him.

I found my thong under the bed, climbed into the rest of my clothes, and made a move for the door. Creeping quietly, my gaze fell on the bowl sitting atop the midcentury modern credenza in the hallway. In it lay a few crumpled bills, a MetroCard, and a folded napkin. I took it and scribbled my name and number on the bottom, under the words I had written the night before: *I want you to give me a massage from the inside.*

One foot out the door, I paused, then snaked my arm back inside and snatched the MetroCard. After all, I couldn't walk away totally empty-handed, not even the first time.

7

HOT DOGS & HAND JOBS

New York was everything I had dreamed it would be—bottled chaos, creative energy, determined hustling, and an escape from everything I had once known and wanted to forget—but like many dreams, mine were being chewed up and shat out by a city that demands the most out of its occupants and accepts nothing less. After seven months, I was keenly aware that I needed to have a real source of income, that even with cheap rent I couldn't subsist solely off petty grifts and the kindness of my roommates, who covered my rent until I could pay them back and didn't notice when I swiped a couple of twenties out of the cup on their dresser that contained their tips from waiting tables.

I started scouring Craigslist's help wanted ads and pored over the "career" section of websites for the cool-kid companies I wanted to work at. Red Bull (the music and events side only),

Vans, Interscope Records, and at the very top of my list: *VICE* magazine.

It was 2008, and *VICE* was in its peak Terry Richardson years (when that was a positive thing) and had moved from its DIY punk origins to being printed in full gloss. Their issues featured hard-hitting news pieces about the war in Afghanistan bookended by ads from Diesel jeans and articles about circumcision. *VICE* was an arbiter in downtown taste and tastelessness; edgy, self-aware, and bold with a DGAF attitude. It was everything I wanted in a job, and it was everything I wanted to be.

Their website didn't list any open positions, but it was easy enough to find the email address of the person in charge—he was, after all, a bit of a celebrity himself. There was an issue of the magazine from a few years prior that was completely dedicated to him, full of interviews with his ex-girlfriends and an editorial shoot where he wore a very European zebra-print pair of underwear, legs spread, while sitting on a child's bed. I crafted a spectacularly witty email, mastered through years of writing and responding to Craigslist ads to cure my boredom, that said *"I'm talented enough to be a staff writer, but I'll also be fine with being an assistant for meager pay."* I reread it a few times, made some tweaks to up the raunchiness, and hit Send with purpose.

A few days passed after I sent *VICE* the cold email and I hadn't heard anything back—nor did I know if I ever would—so I con-

tinued to apply for dozens of other jobs, regardless of being qualified or not. A handful of places responded: a vet clinic looking for
a receptionist, dispatch for a bike messenger company that paid
partially in ounces of marijuana, and an unlisted business where
the interview was set at an address that, when I arrived, ended up
being an abandoned doll factory.

I fantasized about commuting to an office every day, hopefully
one that involved taking the L train into Williamsburg, away from
the auto repair shops of pre–Barclays Center Atlantic Avenue and
the growing parade of strollers in Prospect Heights. In my eyes,
Williamsburg was the land of opportunity, and not just the criminal kind. It was full of music, life, art, and where—even when
I was in Utah—I had always wanted to be. Starved for structure
and routine, most of my friends were trying to get away from the
banality of a traditional nine-to-five, but I knew that a schedule
was my saving grace. My downward spiral needed a plug or I was
going to drown in the dirty dishwater of my life.

Meanwhile, I had taken to the task of reinventing myself
with the same enthusiasm I had for finding a job: hungrily and
lazily. I'd always struggled with extremes, it was always zero or
one hundred, and I had yet to find balance in these dimension-
less numbers—which meant that 50 percent of the time I was
completely detached from reality and subsequently any of the
responsibility that came with it.

Oftentimes my apathy came in handy, because in NYC indifference is one of the most important weapons you can wield. When

you're on the subway and a man walks into your car smelling like a Burning Man port-a-potty, screaming about conspiracy-theory chemtrails and demanding money from you and your fellow passengers, you don't even flinch. He may as well be a used coffee cup rolling around on the ground with the sway of the train. New York is known for being an aggressive city, but in truth, being passive is its superpower.

Though I may not have made the personal vocational advancements I dreamt of, I was certainly becoming more educated. I went to free lectures on every topic you could imagine at famed academic institutions like NYU and Columbia. I walked around Washington Square Park pretending that I had a trust fund instead of targeting those who actually did. I discovered completely new genres of music at shows at the Brooklyn Academy of Music, and I read through every diorama detailing the wonders and blunders of our past on the Museum Mile. The breadth of information available to me was astounding, and I didn't take it for granted.

I also voted for the first time—Barack Obama's inaugural year—and felt the deep reverence of the city on 9/11, seven years after the attack. I was overwhelmed by the gratitude of a place that had become a symbol of hope and resilience for an entire nation. As I walked around Ground Zero I watched tourists take selfies, ear-to-ear smiles plastered on faces in a place that had once seen those same features distorted in immense pain. I was disgusted and enraged for a city that I had barely inhabited but felt very much a citizen of.

My expanded education wasn't limited to lectures and books and exhibits. My street literacy improved through the pedagogy of the School of Hard Knocks. I watched sloppy drunk women drop their purses, the contents exploding on the vomit-stained concrete. Sometimes I rushed to help collect their things, never swiping so much as a hair tie—part misguided feminism, part lack of a challenge—but always took note of how easy it would have been to rob them blind. Pickpockets ran rampant; a targeted bump on the shoulder would distract a hurried commuter as a sly hand slipped into their pocket, wallet gone without a trace. Men dressed as Buddhist monks in goldenrod robes forced their cheap, beaded bracelets into the hands of unsuspecting visitors and would then panhandle aggressively until given a "donation." Street corner hustlers hawked pirated DVDs and fake designer bags that were displayed on the sidewalk, laid on a giant sheet that made it easy to scoop everything up and move when the cops came rushing toward them. Everywhere you looked someone was being swindled.

There were times I'd want to alert the victim of what had transpired. My vision of being a hero blinded me to my own pitfalls (there was rarely a comparison to what the thief was doing and my own actions). But more often than not, I respected the hustler. If some idiot outsider was gullible enough to fall for it, I thought maybe they deserved it. Survival of the fittest in the concrete jungle.

It wasn't only the Times Square con artists who were trying

to make ends meet. Most everyone I knew was struggling finan-
cially, and though we were being ravaged by the economy and our
own egos, if we were going to slum it anywhere during a reces-
sion, this was the place. I met new friends through free concerts
at the Jelly NYC Pool Parties at McCarren Park's then-perma-
drained pool, smoking joints with reckless abandon (the authorities mostly didn't care, but it was still illegal and scratched my itch
to be naughty) while bouncing around to Les Savy Fav, not caring
when ash fell and burnt a hole in the nightgown I was wearing as
a dress. The vibe was wild and chaotic, and above all of it, was so
much fucking fun.

Every generation says that *they* really knew how to party, and
maybe that's true, but eventually if you go back far enough, it
only means everyone was nodding out on heroin. Maybe it was
that we were the last generation to live part of our lives without
the internet, not yet riddled with the anxiety of every moment
being captured and posted. Maybe it was that we were sick of
being the experimental test case for Boomers to raze with their
brazen selfishness, or maybe it was the overwhelming late-stage
capitalism. Whatever the reason may have been, we—the young
degenerates of the aughts—knew how to fucking bring it. Many
of our nights ended in dancing on tables, with revelers doing rails
of shitty drugs off the backs of toilets, off the bars, and off each
other's bodies while the sun came up.

Sometimes I'd go home with one of the skater boys I met at
Enid's and sometimes (but not always) steal shit from him. Fifty

bucks out of his wallet, an iPod inscribed on the back with a message of congratulations for his graduation, a regular-ass pen because I liked the way it glided across the napkins, receipts, and papers that I wrote my stupid messages on that would end up becoming my calling card.

I could have gone *anywhere* to find my marks, but I liked to shit where I ate. Call me old-fashioned, but I needed to feel connected to these men somehow, and I definitely needed to be attracted to them even if I wasn't fucking them (which actually happened far less than most would assume). I often wonder what would have happened if I had gone the sugar baby route, frequenting midtown bars, scoping out men that certainly had more money. I could be sitting in a heated swimming pool in the burbs of Connecticut . . . but what fun is that?

Many of the guys I met were a one-and-done situation, but plenty of them were repeat customers. Those were the ones I thought had boyfriend-worthy qualities and the added bonus that they were exactly like the idiot tourists but even more gullible.

Richie was one of those guys. We met at a Girl Talk concert at Terminal 5 in Hell's Kitchen in the dead of winter, standing in line to check our coats with a hundred other people. It was a very slow-going process—the two surly women manning the station were working at their own pace, and who could blame them really? Even while unemployed I never considered subjecting myself to a job like that regardless of how broke I was.

"Well, the good news is that by the time we check our coats we can get right back in line to pick them up," I heard the guy behind me say good-naturedly.

"That's assuming they don't lose them . . . and the odds don't seem to be in our favor," I replied as I watched the coats pile up on the ground, hangers abandoned. I turned around to see a tall man—handsome in a goofy white-guy way—looking back at me.

"I'm Richard, soon to be coatless," he said.

"Richie, nice to meet you. I'm Kari, soon to be shirtless," I replied brazenly.

"It's *Richard*, and I'm intrigued."

"You can be demoted to Dick if that's your attitude about it."

He made a high-pitched noise, jumbled consonants signaling that we were going back in time, setting us up for a do-over.

"I'm Richie, nice to meet you," he extended his hand.

Two hours later we were dripping with sweat having surrendered ourselves to the music, dancing maniacally in the middle of thousands of others doing the same. Our bodies were pressed together, Richie behind me and holding my waist as I threw my ass in a circle against him. He spun me around so I was looking directly into his hazel eyes and kissed me deeply. His hands started to crawl up my legs slowly, like a vine winding its way up toward the light. Purposefully and without hesitation, his fingers disappeared under my skirt and traced my inner thighs while I shuddered. I closed my eyes and rested my head against his chest as his fingers slipped inside me and a million balloons dropped from the ceiling.

There's nothing more sobering than the harsh fluorescent lights of the subway, and as we began the hour-long journey back to my apartment I studied Richie's face. He was still handsome, but his forehead was sprinkled with acne scars and he had chapped lips (maybe I had sucked all the hydration from them), and he was *very* animated as he spoke. I could tell this was going to annoy me, so I averted my eyes from him as I asked questions about his life and pretended to care.

The conversation eventually turned toward music and I was a bit surprised to find that he actually knew his shit. We bounced names of producers and songwriters off one another and discussed the cultural significance of Outkast's *Southernplayalisticadillac-muzik*. While we were waxing poetic about how crazy it was that we were both listening to Radiohead the first time we did mushrooms (which is not a rarity, as I've found out over the years), I decided Richie was going to be a regular-ass one night stand. One void of any nefarious intent—a normal coupling like any normal person might have. It was normal to be simultaneously annoyed and drawn to a person you'll never see again. This was all normal. *I* was normal.

"Thanks for letting me crash at your place," he said, filling the space during a short lull in conversation.

"I should warn you that 'my place' is not only mine. I have a bunch of roommates."

"Cool," he said without missing a beat.

"Wait," I paused. "Where would you have stayed if not with me?"

"Uh, well, hmm," he pondered.

"Oh my god, you *planned* on meeting someone tonight! This is a premeditated flirter."

"I mean, I guess I hadn't . . . yeah. You got me." He put his hands up, mocking an arrest. "But I'm really glad it ended up being you," he added.

I reconsidered the regular-ass-ness of this situation. Was I the one being taken advantage of?

Forcing a smile, I agreed. "Yeah, me too."

"Hey, how's it going?"

My roommate Jared snuck up on me as I was zoned out, staring through our small kitchen window at a cyclone of trash whirling around our neighbor's overgrown yard. My head whipped around as fast as the dead leaves and hair outside.

"Jared! Good morning!" I said in a far too enthusiastic way that made it clear that I was overcompensating for something.

He gave me a strange smile. "So, you got in pretty late last night . . ."

"Did I? Was I too loud?"

"I heard panting." The strange smile persisted.

"You know how that last flight of stairs really takes it out of me."

He winked knowingly and thankfully changed the subject. It's not that I didn't want him to know about my sexual escapades; I just wasn't in the mood to chat about Richie's limp whiskey dick and how I faked an orgasm so intense that I was basically moaning, *"I should be stealing from you."*

"We got the electricity bill," Jared said. "ConEd is fucked. It's $200 more than it was last month. I'm gonna pay for it but if you can give me your part by the end of this week . . ."

"For sure, I'll get cash tomorrow," I said.

"How's the job hunt going?" he asked.

"Oh, you know, the possibilities are endless. Amateur night at PUMPS, amateur foot fetish parties, amateur hour at the clown car factory. How much do you think I could make off these suckers?"

I looked at my feet and wiggled my toes as if using them for the first time.

"Listen, Kari, the roomies and I were talking and . . ."

Oh, shit—this was it. They had me figured out. My heart began to race and flashbacks of being cornered in the bathroom in Salt Lake City invaded my mind.

". . . we love you and were wondering if you wanted to move into the fifth bedroom."

Relief flooded over my entire body. Followed by confusion.

"Wait, there's a fifth bedroom?"

A week later, Alec, the roommate I was subletting my room from, returned from his tour and I moved my suitcase across the hallway and into the "fifth bedroom": a walk-in closet next to the front door. It was big enough for a single bed, which I had bought from IKEA and put together, body smashed up against the wall.

I was thrilled. My rent had somehow gotten even cheaper, and I had a couple of legit interviews lined up with a software company and Avon's corporate office. Things were looking up!

I, of course, was still luring bearded dudes into my web at Rbar, going home with them, and then leaving with their cash while all they were left with were blue balls. At the time it felt like survival, and I suppose in ways it was, but not like how most people think of it. Survival for me wasn't so much about how I was going to pay for my next meal, but how I was going to get through the entirety of my life *being me*. I felt trapped in my head and was desperate to find a way out, and after ignoring the fact that there might not be an escape hatch, I was thrown into a deep depression that made me lazy. By being so future-forward I neglected the now. It was, like so much of my life had been, a solitary experience.

I had started to put the pieces together, albeit slowly, that what I was doing wasn't okay. I had always *known* that, but I began to acknowledge it within myself, trying to pull out of my delusions. And even though I could pump the brakes, I wasn't able to come to a full stop. Richie had ultimately won me over, and we were talking nearly every day, but I had added a handful of other un-witting men to my roster underneath his nose. It was exhausting juggling all of them, and sometimes things got jumbled up: a sext meant for Andrew (*"I want you dripping down my thighs"*) would get sent to Josh while we were planning a weekend bike ride to The Cloisters.

Late one night, while at my apartment with Richie, pressed against each other in my closet, I got a call.

JOSH ST JEROMES flashed on my screen. I quickly sent it to voicemail and placed my phone face down on the floor.

"Four in the morning seems a little late for a call," Richie said rigidly.

"Spam calls know no schedule, *Richard.* They don't subjugate themselves to the division of time set by mere mortals!" I said with bravado, trying to make him laugh.

Making people laugh means they trust you. I needed him to laugh.

He didn't and instead reached over my body and quickly swiped my phone off the ground.

"Hey! Come on! What are you doing?"

"Unlock it," he demanded, holding the screen toward me.

I stared at him coldly, willing him to break eye contact, even if only for a second. Once he did I'd have control over the situation, over him. Like dogs in the wild.

"Unlock. It."

I sucked on the insides of my cheeks. I was playing fierce, but internally I was cycling through the emotional up and downs I had come to expect, but that never got easier. I was surprised he couldn't see my heart beating through my shirt.

He tapped on the screen and I heard the *click* that indicated the phone had been unlocked.

"8008? Really? Boob?"

"I like them, what can I say? You're not going to find anything in there," I said softly.

I consulted my playbook: when aggressiveness fails, you play submissive. Roll over halfway, attempt to extinguish the situation before it ignites. Make them feel bad about ever mistrusting you. Be angry, let them beg.

He held the screen up to me again to show me my recent calls.

ANDREW TALL DARKROOM

Mark???

Austin DBA

JOSH McKibben

"Richie, *look*, all of these are missed calls. That's what the red means, baby," I said patiently and with a hint of patronization.

His expression softened a bit, "But why are they calling you?"

"Are you saying that I shouldn't be the object of all their affection?" I spat out, and before he could interject I continued. "They're, like, obsessed with me. But I don't answer, because I'm *your* object of affection."

I climbed on top of Richie and started kissing him forcefully. As I started rocking my hips back and forth I gently took my phone back. I slid it between the bed and the wall and made a mental note to change my passcode.

He flipped me over and pushed himself into me with force.

"I bet Andrew and Tim can't fuck you as good as I can," he grunted.

"No, baby, I'll answer your call anytime," I growled as I grabbed his hand and put it around my throat.

Even though I was fucking with all these boys, when I actually dreamt about being in a real relationship—the kind I knew my brain would never allow me to have, the kind that required trust—it was with a woman.

From the time I was in elementary school, staring at my tow-headed crush (whom I asked so often to borrow her ChapStick she ended up just giving it to me), I always wanted the affection and attention of a woman. Abandonment issues, much? Women were complicated and I didn't understand them. I stood in awe, worshiped them, but didn't know how to talk to them. I stood there twiddling my thumbs, waiting for a smart, funny girl to write *me* a stupid note on a napkin.

I met Julia around the same time I met Richie, through a mutual friend. She was wacky and driven, and stunning in an unconventional way with her thick black hipster glasses and racially ambiguous face (sometimes she told people she was Filipino and other times German or Mexican). She possessed an awkward confidence and felt like the realest person I knew, and I was immediately smitten.

Julia and her roommates lived in Greenpoint, Brooklyn, before it was filled with fancy coffee shops and rock-climbing gyms, when it was difficult to find a restaurant that didn't serve Polish food, and none of the buildings had elevators. Their decrepit walk-up stood on Calyer Street, and when ascending to the fifth floor you had to be certain to skip specific stairs, otherwise you'd find yourself plummeting into the basement below.

Julia's apartment was one of life and creativity: a drum set shoved into one corner of the living room, an easel in the opposite corner, a single stool serving its purpose for both pursuits. Her room was small but comfortable and she had strung up lights that gave off the perfect ambience.

We became close friends quickly, and I was really trying to be honest with her. At least in the beginning. With Julia I could identify the lies before they came out of my mouth, and I'd shove them back down, with great satisfaction. This was progress. Julia was good for me. At least in the beginning. Up until this point I hadn't had many positive female relationships in my life, and ours felt warm and comfortable and true.

Julia and I hung out a lot, and there were periods of time where I didn't go home for days. I'd borrow her clothes and lounge on the couch while she was at work, smelling her shampoo that lingered on the hood of the sweatshirt I was wrapped up in. I'd daydream that I really lived there, that Julia was my girlfriend, and that we were happy and in love.

Julia's roommates were equally as gracious and fun. I could see why they all wanted to live with one another, beyond the trifurcation of rent. They were a real family, sharing space, meals, responsibilities, and lives. They quarreled but never fought, they were free from unnecessary drama. They truly cared for one another and soon I was cared for by them, too.

A lot of parties were held on Calyer, and it was rare for a weekend to go by without a room full of people jumping to the beat of too-loud music, pushing the limits of the weak framework of the house. It was at one such party that Julia entered with a tall man in tow.

"EVERYONE!" she shouted over the music. "This is Tim!"

I watched as they walked in, Tim following Julia like a puppy, weaving through people in between hugs and how-are-yous. In the kitchen they each took a shot of tequila, Julia's face red and happy as she poured Tim another one and tipped it back into his mouth. I turned away and busied myself by collecting abandoned beers and wiping condensation off the tables, trying to collect my thoughts. How stupid was I to think that we could be anything more than friends? I knew Julia wasn't, like, *straight-straight*, but I had no idea how curved her rainbow was. And did I even want to *be* with her, or did I only like being with her? Maybe this was a good thing—she seemed happy—and all I ever wanted was for my friends to be happy, right? No, wrong. I wouldn't have done the things I had if that were the case. I blinked rapidly, a side effect of neurons firing haphazardly when I was overwhelmed, and I slammed my eyelids down to try to quiet the world.

A tap on the shoulder sent me into a tailspin, but I held on to the edge of sanity with a death grip and slowly turned around with a smile.

"Kari! This is Tim," Julia announced as if I hadn't heard her say that when they first arrived. "He's the one I've been telling you about."

She had not.

"Hi, Tim. I've heard so many bad things about you. Crazy what you did to that boy in the second grade." I smiled.

"Kari's jealous that I brush my hair for you," Julia interjected.

"Sure am. Nice to meet you."

Tim and I shook hands and Julia told us to sit tight while she went to get more shots for the two of them.

"Soooooo . . . you're a little hostile," Tim said.

An honest laugh escaped from my lips. He got me.

"Hmm, maybe," I mused, "or protective."

He eyed me and was about to say something when Julia bounded back and shoved another glass of liquid in his face.

"Drink up, the night is young!" she yelled as she turned the music up even louder.

Over the next couple of weeks, I saw a lot of Tim. He was fine, nothing overtly offensive about him, but Julia deserved so much more than what he had to offer. Someone daring, someone complicated, someone who believed in her. Instead she was doing *fine*.

I was able to contain my jealousy for the most part, but it

poured over one day when she told me that we needed to reschedule a movie night because Tim's family was going to be in town and she would be meeting his parents.

"Seems a little soon for that, no?" I prodded.

"Seems a little old-fashioned to adhere to norms instituted by the patriarchy, no?"

I stared at her and pretended to be upset that she was questioning my integrity, something that barely existed.

"You know what," I said, "go and meet his parents. I'm really so happy for you." Tears welled up in my eyes.

"Whoa, are you okay?" Julia asked. "What's wrong?"

"No, I'm sorry . . . I . . . I've been having a hard time recently. Some . . . health issues have come up . . . and I haven't wanted anyone to worry about me."

"Oh my god, what's going on?" she asked with real concern. I had her undivided attention.

Over the next few days I teased out a fraudulent life-threatening illness. One that was made more believable by two trips to the emergency room. Complaints of phantom pain that ultimately became real in the form of stomach ulcers that felt like they were eating me alive, my guilt manifesting itself in peptic revolt.

Julia held my hand in the ER, being careful to not disturb the clear plastic tube of the IV catheter coming out of it, and told me that she would always be there for me. I smiled and let the warmth of the pain meds envelop me as I quietly told her I loved her.

Julia never met Tim's parents. Their short trip came and went while she dutifully tended to me, and when they eventually broke up the lung cancer I had lied about went into remission.

One evening, a few days after I got out of the hospital, the roomies and I were crammed into Jared's room watching the most recent episode of *True Blood* (*Suuuuuuuukiii*) when my iPhone *dinged*. I saw a notification for an email pop up, sent from *VICE*, and my life literally changed forever.

I shot up and ran to my closet room, shutting the door clumsily behind me. I tapped my phone and let out a triumphant yelp as I read that *VICE* wanted me to come in the following week for an interview. I went to respond and stopped myself short. No one likes someone who's *too* eager. After the appropriate amount of time (which in this case was ten minutes), I solidified a date and time and went back to Jared's room to share the happy news.

After a weekend that went by far too slowly, the day of the interview had finally arrived. I spun around 360 degrees like a pinwheel in a hurricane, pulling clothes off hangers, off my bed, and throwing them all onto the floor. I had to leave in thirty minutes and I still hadn't decided what to wear.

Searching for inspiration, I anxiously flipped through the most recent issue of the print magazine of *VICE* (free for the taking, stacked by the doors of the coolest stores and bars, often next to *The Village Voice* and a fishbowl of NYC Health Department–branded condoms). I stopped on the Dos and Don'ts section toward the back—a fan-favorite feature that critiqued fashion choices by way of telling hot girls they were hot and referring to everyone else with an outdated, offensive slur—and decided on an outfit that said *"Jenny Lewis on the streets, Karen O in the sheets."* I quickly drew too-thick liner on my eyes, slapped some blush on my cheeks, grabbed my résumé (in a transparent purple paper protector I swiped from OfficeMax), and ran out the door.

Rumbling through Williamsburg on the B48 bus, I read up on conjoined twins, the going rate of heroin in Tunisia, and the latest on the Bernie Madoff investment scandal. I had no idea what to expect from this interview, but I wanted to be prepared.

A text popped up: *Good luck today, babe!*

Oh, Richie. He wouldn't be wishing for my prosperity if only he knew that as soon as I could take myself out to dinner I planned on kicking him to the curb.

Nearing the corner of North 10th and Berry Street, I pulled the taut yellow cord and exited the bus with a little hop. Slowly walking up the block, eyes peeled for the address, I took a deep breath and told myself I was going to kill the interview. I looked up at the building before me, *VICE* logo on the door, and flung it open.

I checked in with the front desk person and was led to a glass office that was in the middle of the large open floor plan. The heels of my black "rock star" boots clicked loudly on the industrial-chic polished concrete floor. A few too-cool-looking employees gazed up from their computers apathetically, probably wondering why I wasn't delivering them lines of cocaine on a silver platter or whatever other debaucherous things happened within these walls. The air felt electric in its indifference.

I sat waiting patiently, thinking about how I was here, in an office I could have only dreamt of, to interview for a job that I had basically manifested. I was proud of the obstacles I had overcome, and envisioned a life free of compulsive lying, liberation from balancing dualities that had been born out of spite of one another.

As I was patting myself on the back for making it this far, a plain-looking white guy entered the office. He sat down without shaking my hand even though I had stood up and extended mine.

"So, you *are* Asian. Does that mean you can also balance nine spinning plates while creating a spreadsheet?" he asked, referencing lines from my email.

The rest of the interview was quick and easy. I rattled off my experience, citing the former companies I hadn't worked for that filled my résumé. I threw in an anecdote about an upset client I had calmed down, a Plan B I had come up with when a rainstorm threatened a large-scale festival, how I didn't mind getting my hands dirty. Besides, I knew that *had* I been in those situations, that's what I would've done, so it was easy to sell. Being persuasive is a transferable skill, after all.

The interviewer, who I learned was the head publisher, and I got along great. My usual character flaws and deceptions were fine print at the bottom of a page full of positive qualities. There to be seen, but mostly ignored. It felt good to sell myself like this.

"So when can you start?" he asked.

*   *   *

After the interview I giddily floated down the block to McCarren Park and sat on a bench to watch a baseball game where the outfielders smoked cigarettes as they trotted toward the ball in their tight jeans and ironic tees. The sun shone brightly through the cool spring air, balmy enough that I removed my jacket and exposed my bare arms. I let the warmth envelop me, and through closed eyes my future looked bright.

Later, I burst through the door of the apartment, overflowing with my good news.

"JARED! ARE YOU HOME?"

He came rushing out of his room, hair disheveled, clearly woken up from slumber by my squeals.

"What's going on? Are you okay?"

I threw a few hundred-dollar bills his way with a laugh.

"I am the ultimate hipster now. I got the job!"

He hugged me and we bounced up and down while holding on to one another until he said that he was going back to bed, and gave a little fist pump before heading to his room.

I leaned against the wall and unlocked my phone and scrolled through my texts. Richie's message sat unanswered. I tapped through to his contact info and quickly blocked his number.

This was it: the beginning of my new life, the new me.

8

CAPTURE

I was on top of the fucking world. I had done it. Fake it until you make it, baby! And hadn't I been doing exactly that my entire life? I faked being white, faked being a good Mormon girl, faked being straight. But those chains were broken, and here the fuck I was. Feeling invigorated, I opened the door to my new possibilities with a swift kick that set the fire alarms off.

Having a job at *VICE* felt amazing, despite the poor pay and long hours. I was tasked with general executive assistant work: managing schedules, processing invoices, responding to emails from people wondering when their invoices would be processed, and sending orders out to the printers. It was menial work that didn't take a lot of brain power, but it didn't matter to me. I would have been happy to suck on a cigarette and blow the smoke into my boss's mouth if that's what had been asked of me.

My coworkers were as plugged in and cool as I imagined they'd be. On Monday mornings it wasn't rare to see everyone riding in on the struggle bus; tales of crazy loft parties and hallucinogens that hadn't quite worn off yet were shared around the watercooler. If I had gotten that other job at Avon I'd likely be talking about someone's stupid-ass baby, pretending to give a shit that they took their first steps. Instead, I got to cheer on the last steps of a wild Saturday out that a man-child could remember.

Despite the rad new job (we still said things like "rad" back then), my old habits were hard to break. When my new colleagues asked about my own life, I stuck to the half-truths listed on my résumé. I started school at the University of Utah and transferred to NYU. I had worked at a major events production company, but they didn't have offices in New York. Etc., etc., etc. If only I had known and accepted that my actual genesis was far more interesting than some bullshit academia. But there I was, stretching the truth so thin that it sagged like an old man's scrotum.

I also almost immediately started using my new job for clout. Julia was a fledgling writer, so I told her I might be able to get her a copywriting gig. I told friends of friends I could set up meetings for them with the editors. And I told *everyone* that I could give them coveted plus-ones to various events and parties. "Email me," I'd say, happy to spell my name slowly, emphasizing the domain: *at viceland.com*. I loved the way that it felt in my mouth, the snake-like hiss into the soft unfurling of my tongue against my top row of teeth.

As one could expect—this was *VICE* after all—the cool factor came at the expense of a highly toxic environment. Especially so for a woman, and *especially* for one of color. One time, during a meeting where the team was discussing a potential recurring feature tentatively titled *Weird Shit Eaten in Asia*, the staff writers looked over at me.

"Kari, you're Asian, right?" a statement that came out like a question—never a good sign.

I looked up from my notes. "That's what I've been told. Haven't taken a DNA test yet though."

"Okay, so, what weird, gross food did you eat growing up?" he asked nonchalantly.

"Umm . . . lots of casseroles. Oh, definitely carrots in Jell-o. It's kind of a Utah thing."

"So," he paused. "You didn't eat, like, dog or horse or anything particularly nasty?"

Flashes of playground bullies and that bitch from the hibachi restaurant danced across my mind, and I flinched from the heat of my embarrassment. I recovered quickly with a smile to seem easygoing in the face of not-so-casual racism, and chuckled along with the rest of my coworkers.

Other days, I spent my time looking through pages and pages of photos of young girls holding their tops up, flashing the camera with reckless abandon, searching for the right one for a spread. Unsurprisingly, the model was never credited, only the photographer (who was most likely some dude with a ridiculous mustache). Maybe that was for the best. At the time, this kind of work seemed like a perk, and I would brag to my friends that it was better than having health insurance. Besides, I'd rather be doing that than looking through the photos of hairy balls that also graced the publication.

Two weeks after I had started at *VICE*, I was on the same B48 that had taken me to my interview, heading the opposite way, deeper into Brooklyn. I was en route to the apartment of a guy I had met one Saturday night at a dance party in the sweaty back room of Royal Oak.

As the bus rocked and rolled over potholes and asphalt cavities, I told myself that *today* was the day that I was going to start being truthful—besides, there wasn't even that much I'd have to backpedal on. I could just Start. Being. Honest. It was something I had tried to hold myself to since I'd started hanging out with this guy—I really liked him—but continuously failed, as little lies would slip out, escaping from between my lips like a sardine coated in oil.

Staring at my phone, I read posts on a website called Gothamist that focused on New York City news and pop culture (which is its own universe, infinitely more entertaining than regular news). I scrolled quickly past blurbs of shady politicians, near-sexual photos of pizza with stringy, gooey cheese from the Best Slice Shops of 2009, when a familiar face quickly flashed on my screen.

I sucked in a sharp breath and with a defiant thumb stopped the words and images that whizzed by. I slowly crept back up the page as my heart started to beat faster.

Not for a second did I think, *Oh wow! That girl looks like we could be sisters.* I was deeply familiar with my own mug shot and recognized it immediately. I had purchased a high-resolution print of it, after all. Something like panic rose in my throat. I couldn't process *how* worried I should be, only that this was very not good.

Around my mug shot was a thick blue border, with bright-red letters that spelled out MOST WANTED. *Oh,* I thought. *This is very, very not good.*

Above the phone number that people were asked to call if they had any information was a laundry list of my charges. I was wanted on five warrants totaling $60,000 for "forgery, bad checks, and retail theft."

I looked around at the other passengers. They were none the wiser, but I shrank in my seat and pulled my jacket collar higher over my face anyway. I jumped off the bus at the next stop and ran across the street to catch the one that would take me back home.

I later learned that earlier that day, *VICE* had posted a public "memo" from "The Department of Oopsies," after they had discovered that one of their executive assistants was a fugitive, encouraging everyone to google their prospective employees before hiring them. This hot tip was as far as their HR professionalism went, and I never heard from anyone from the company again (and, in fact, I think they still owe *me* money).

News got around fast. Gothamist had pulled the story from a much larger one in *The New York Observer*, where the author bestowed upon me the catchy moniker I'd come to be known by for the rest of my life: *Hipster Grifter.*

As word spread, text message after text message poured in.

WTF?!

Is this u??

So you don't have cancer, you lying bitch?

The dings were like bullets in my chest, each one causing a shudder to rip through my body, but the last one, from Julia, broke me into a million pieces.

Over the next couple of days things really went gangbusters. Multiple news and gossip outlets picked up the story, but none took as obsessive an interest as Gawker.com, a site dedicated to pop culture, celebs, and New York media, aka the *literati.* Gawker was making multiple posts about me—rarely referring to me as anything but Hipster Grifter—sometimes up to three to four a day. There were interviews with past "boyfriends," leaked nudes (which *The Philadelphia Inquirer* actually fucking linked people to), guesses as to why I did what I did, and most importantly where I was located now.

People were submitting sightings of me to Gawker Stalker and the NYPD. My email was blowing up with inquiries from reporters. A Google search for "hipster grifter" brought up thousands of tweets and countless articles from across the nation (and a handful of international mentions—one from Italy is particularly memorable, referring to me as "The Filth"). Napkins and match-books I had written on were being sold on eBay; someone made fake action movie posters with my face superimposed over the lead star that were being wheatpasted around Brooklyn; there were T-shirts and paper dolls and bingo cards.

Though a lot of what was being said was true, there was a fair amount of nonfactual information in the mix. My name was spelled a number of ways, my age varied by two to four years, the amount of money I had stolen ballooned up to $150,000, but it didn't matter—no one was paying attention to those details. No one cared that it was my *warrants* that totaled $60,000, I hadn't *stolen* $60,000 (call me an egoist, but the tens of thousands of dollars' difference matters to me). No one cared that there was a person behind the memes.

All people wanted to focus on was my race (subservient Asian gone bad!) and sexuality (she's a crazy slut down for anything!). It obviously didn't help that I had used those two stereotypes to my advantage to con so many people. The story had all the snappy features of what makes true crime fascinating to so many people, years before the genre really exploded. Twitter had only existed for a short period of time, and virality was a new concept that people were really latching on to. My head spun as I read all of the horrifying comments and tweets.

I had the wherewithal to realize that my roommates and the rest of my friends were going to figure out who I was very quickly. So, I planned on doing what I did best: I was going to disappear. I grabbed the giant suitcase out of my closet room and stuffed my meager belongings into it, a mere few months after they were suffocated inside the first time. I looked at my small bed, the one that would have to be chopped up into smaller pieces to get it out of the room, and thought, *Here it is, my lasting legacy*. Before I walked out for the last time, I grabbed a Sharpie and lay on my back, scrawling my name and the year on the underside of the bed frame. No one may ever see it, I thought, but at least I knew I was there.

With the speed of a desperate person on the lam, I got a job as a live-in assistant in Bed-Stuy off Craigslist (using a fake last name, natch), and after a few emails back and forth and a phone call, the gig was mine. An unassuming friend of mine who didn't know what was going on agreed to pick me up and pay for a cab to move me to my new place. Or did I run out of the cab, leaving him to foot the bill? I can't quite remember, but it was the last time I saw him.

The apartment was a fifth-floor walk-up, past doors so thin they may as well not have been there. Crying babies, screaming couples, basketball commentators on the TV—you could hear every screeching word. I struggled with my suitcase up the stairs, sweat beading on my face as I lugged it the last few steps.

After catching my breath for a second, I knocked tentatively on the door of my new home and waited. No response. I knocked again with a little more oomph. Nothing. My thoughts started to race as I looked around the hallway, wondering if I was being set up. Was someone watching me? There *was* a guy who was walking suspiciously close to me earlier in the day.

I was startled when my thoughts of being in a James Patterson spy-thriller were interrupted. The door swung open with a *THWACK* as it hit my suitcase. A man in his late thirties stood against the jamb, half-smiling, not speaking.

"Um hey," I said. "I'm Kari. Thanks again for letting me stay here."

"I'm not *letting* you do anything. You'll be earning it."

The hair on the back of my neck bristled, and I wondered if it would be easier to throw myself over the railing of the winding staircase and end it. Ugh, but if I didn't die I'd end up in the hospital and eventually in custody, potentially without the use of my legs. I'd take my chances.

"Oh God, that came out wrong," he said. "I didn't mean it like, you know, like in a gross way. I'm excited to have a competent assistant for once. I'm Carter."

He extended his arm and opened the door farther. "Come on in. I'll show you your new digs."

The apartment was much cleaner than I had anticipated, based on the fact that its inhabitant was the kind of man who hires someone off Craigslist and then lets them occupy his living space. The walls were bare besides a couple of framed photos that were hung haphazardly, unoccupied nails dotted around them. At some point there had been a lot more pictures.

A bright red IKEA couch sat in the living room, the color popping next to the contrast of the nothingness, almost like an unexpected scream. Next to it was a desk with a monitor, and a

Dell computer on the floor (the tower kind that I used to turn on with my toe as a kid).

"Welcome to your office," he said, gesturing toward the desk.

I had been hired to help Carter with his business, WebPage-Polisher, which created and maintained websites for other companies. My main job was to manage communication with customers and drum up new business, while Carter actually built and coded the sites.

"We have three clients right now who are pretty much self-serving, but we need . . . a lot more of them. To be honest, we're struggling a bit, so I'm really happy to have a helping hand, and we can take this to the next level," he said earnestly.

The hair on my neck had relaxed and I started to warm up to him. After all, we were basically business partners now.

"So I hope you don't mind, but your room is my daughter's." He paused. "But she's only here a handful of days out of the month. She normally wants to sleep in my room anyway."

I sensed his sadness and that warmed me to him even more. Two tortured souls creating a way out . . . toward what? Who knows. But we would do it together. Partners.

"What's her name?"

"Juniper. My baby."

I misheard him, and excitedly exclaimed, "I love astronomy!"

He cocked his head and looked like he was about to correct me, but didn't.

"You can move her toys, shift things around, whatever you

want. Maybe you can meet her one of these days," he said wist-fully. And then, "Alright, I'll leave you to it. Come on out when you're ready and we can start going over the software."

I sat down on the small bed, low to the ground, not too dissimilar from the one that had been trapped in the closet. I closed my eyes and thought about how this was my *second* New York apartment. I told myself that I was still standing against all odds and tried to convince myself that being surrounded by stuffed animals and sparkly dream catchers in a roach-infested building was an upgrade.

Over the next day I got up to speed on the business, which was fine in theory, but I soon learned was otherwise a total disaster. Carter was talented but disorganized. He couldn't keep his projects straight, and more than once sent an email to the wrong client, and then asked me to explain the mishap to them and try to upgrade their level of service. He loved to email me, even though he could have asked for whatever he needed through the paper-thin walls. But I didn't mind. It felt professional.

We would wake up, plan for the day, and execute . . . to vary-ing degrees of success. In my first week we got two new customers from a Craigslist ad I wrote. Things felt like they were getting better. Being good at the job made it easier to ignore the fact that I hadn't gone outside in days, and I tried not to think about the mug shot or the emails piling up in my personal inbox asking where the fuck I was.

On my third day, there was a loud knock on the door, and

I froze in my chair, hands hovering over the keyboard. Carter's head popped around the corner and he put his finger to his lips.

"Carter, I know you're in there!" a voice boomed, one that I sensed was coming from a large man who had little tolerance for bullshit. Carter was biting his lip aggressively—something he did a lot—and shaking his head, willing me to stay silent. Oh, if he even knew how far I'd go to avoid speaking to an authoritarian figure banging on a door . . .

"You have until the end of this week, Carter! Four days. Four grand."

With a final bang on the door, seemingly sealing Carter's fate, we heard the stairs groan under the loud man's weight as he descended.

"What the fuck, Carter? Who was that?" I whisper-screamed.

"My landlord. Nice guy, real nice guy, actually. Until he isn't."

"You owe him four thousand dollars?" I asked, as if I wasn't in the same predicament.

"More than that, but he's letting me do it in payments."

"How are you going to get the money?" I asked. We barely had enough funds to test one Facebook ad and we weren't getting any return on it.

"I'll figure it out. Always do. Let's get back to work."

Over the next two days we hustled as hard as we could, but since I didn't know what Carter's exact financial situation was, I also didn't know if the words he was repeating throughout the day were reassurance or a bad omen: *We're close, we're close.*

On the eve of the fourth day we ate $1 egg rolls from the Chinese place down on the corner that someone once got stabbed in, the blood staining the cement for weeks after. The only noise in the quiet room was the crunch of the delicious, flaky deep-fried logs. I wanted to ask what was going to happen, but was scared to hear the answer. I knew that my past was catching up to me, as well as the police. But, as per usual, I was being a giant fucking pussy. I'd rather lie about money and having cancer than confront anyone or myself. So I kept crunching.

I knew that Carter wasn't in a good place, and that he was worried for his daughter and for himself. My heart ached for him. He truly was such a kind man who deserved great success, but I was so caught up in my own shit that I didn't have the capacity for much beyond the thought. I'd been told that's what really counted, anyway. We finished eating and Carter and I shared a silent hug before going to bed.

Later that night in the dead of sleep, I shot up, woken by an intense dream in which I was driving a car, desperately pumping the brakes to no avail, while it continued to gain speed. I looked up at the road, and my panic increased even though there was only open sky ahead, no giant crates stamped ACME in the middle of the road, no speed bumps, only vast desert.

I padded to the bathroom to wash the blood out of my mouth from clenching my jaw so tightly and noticed Carter's bedroom door ajar with the light on. *What time is it?* I wondered. I spat and rinsed the sink out, catching myself in the mirror. A scared creature looked back at me, eyes wide and exhausted. I barely recognized myself, even though internally I hadn't for years, and shakily stepped away from the mirror and my shocked appearance. *Fuck. What has happened to me?*

Back in Juniper's room I glanced at the pink-and-white Minnie Mouse clock on the dresser. The shorter gloved hand pointed toward the three. Carter must be working down to the wire. Oh, how I hoped things would work out for him, for us. I had a few more hours to toss and turn, and dejectedly fell back asleep. As bad as my stress dreams were, they didn't come close to the actual horrors of my real life.

In the morning I arose, not to the usual aroma of Carter's gigantic mug of Folger's (the best part of waking up), but to a sickly silent apartment. I knew immediately that Carter was gone. I cautiously walked into his room to confirm his absence and found a note on the bed.

Kari—

Had to go back to Texas. Think you'll understand. Feel free to stay in the apartment until you can't anymore. Hope to see you in the future.

—Carter

I sat on the bed and tried to force some kind of emotional release, but the tears wouldn't come.

A few days later, after surviving off bodega bagels with butter and twenty-five-cent Utz potato chips, I knew I couldn't do it anymore. I had to go back home to Utah to take care of my shit, to clean up some of the wreckage I had left in my wake, even if it meant going back to jail.

Now, there are a few versions of how I eventually found myself behind bars for the long haul.

The first is that I went to Philadelphia—in an attempt to avoid the NY media shitshow—and turned myself in. The second is that I went to Philadelphia, lured there by a friend, who then handed me over to the police. The third version, the true one, is that it was a bit of both.

I decided to go to Philly because a guy I knew was in a band that was soon embarking on a US tour and was scheduled to play a show at Kilby Court in Salt Lake City. My plan was I'd tag along in their smelly, cramped white van and have a bit of a final cross-country hurrah, parting ways once we got to Utah. They would head to California, and I would head to the local precinct. At least that's what I kept telling myself the plan was, but my track record for doing things I said I would was almost always a losing bet.

Ultimately, I didn't have to make that decision. Once I stepped off the Chinatown Bolt Bus on 30th Street, I was apprehended by multiple officers from the Philadelphia Police Department. My large suitcase, packed yet again with all of my belongings, was taken in as evidence. There's a photo from that night where I'm shown flanked by officers as they led me to a cop car out of frame, a slight smile playing across my lips. There was a lot of discussion as to why I reacted that way, with most guessing it was because I was a fucking psychopath.

In reality, it was an expression of pure relief.

9

RIOT GRRRL

"Holy fuck, this is actually happening." I raised my lunch tray to shield my face, blocking the onslaught of starchy projectiles and small, hard plastic cups typically reserved for children and mentally unstable adults. We fell into both categories.

As I frantically swung around to protect myself, I saw four inmates charging toward me. I braced myself for impact, but at the last minute they sidestepped me with a *"Get the fuck out of the way!"* and slammed into the double-paned glass wall that separated us from our freedom, all balled fists and curse words I couldn't make out.

"LOCKDOWN, NOW!" a guard shouted over the intercom. His voice projected from a carceral Tower of Babel that overlooked our pod, looming one floor above us with its one-way windows, intimidating us with the reflection of our own faces.

"If you do not comply, there will be disciplinary measures. DO YOU UNDERSTAND?!"

Spades, an inmate who identified as a boy when in jail but as a girl on the outs, shuffled around me, their buzzcut head bobbing up and down in glee. They were smiling maniacally, clearly enjoying the chaos. As they threw their weight around with reckless abandon, a garbage can flew overhead. Spades swiped at the abandoned sporks on the table and sent them flying across the room.

"Don't worry Chee-na," they said. "I always protect my girls."

That's what I was called here, *Chee-na*. "China" with a lilted Hispanic accent. Even in this place, stripped of all pretense, I had a mistaken identity. With a wink, Spades promised me I'd be waived the customary two nutty bars and a noodle protection fee. I nodded even though I knew I'd have to pay up one way or another. Everything in jail was for sale—and I mean *everything*—and there was a fuckload of fine print attached.

At this particular point in time, however, it didn't matter. I would do what I had to do to settle my debt later. Truth is, I was fucking terrified and the total pandemonium of the situation had me frozen in place. A place that was quickly starting to resemble a war zone.

I trailed closely behind Spades as they guided me around bolted-down stainless-steel tables and we climbed the stairs toward the safety of my upper-level cell. Spades paused on the way up, taking a moment to point an accusatory finger toward the guards hidden in the tower.

"You know what you did," Spades said, watching their own reflection mouth the words back at them.

Baby's First Riot was a vibrant splash of chaos in our otherwise banal lives. The days leading up to the anarchy plodded along, like each one before it: slow stampede, step after shackled step toward court dates, mail call, and the library cart. I had been in the Riverside Correctional Facility in Northeast Philadelphia for close to thirty days. The first few were a whirlwind—things happened so fast that reality slowed down, like in movies where the main character is about to pass out, nearby voices starting to fade as they are eaten up by the all-encompassing silence of the unknown.

Much like they were in Utah, my possessions were confiscated immediately and I was given a few meager items in exchange: the standard uniform (this time in light blue), a sliver of soap, a washcloth, a ragged towel, a no-name brand of travel-sized toothpaste, and the hard bristles it should be applied to. I was relieved that I had navigated this process before, that I wasn't going into it completely blind. There was a strange comfort in spotting the similarities between my first jail experience and this new one, which was such a depressing thought that I'd spiral into a cyclical mindfuck of being grateful and then terrified that I was. My internal meltdown was interrupted by my cellie, a first-timer, who let out a loud and painful sob during intake. I gripped my fingers tightly around the itchy taxpayer-funded blanket and continued to watch the hands on the clock orbit.

We were being held in the general population "receiving pod," where we had to stay until our tuberculosis tests came back negative. Every morning at 6:00 A.M. a guard would come around as the inmates lazily stuck their arms out for inspection. If the bump at the injection site, administered with a quick prick upon our arrival, hadn't grown, they moved on. If it was raised or hard, they told you to get back into the cell and close the door. Eventually those people would be picked up and taken to the infirmary where . . . I guess they recovered from TB?

Whatever the case, I passed with flying colors (I've always been good at tests *hair flip*) and on the third day I was moved to a more permanent pod. Like the first day back to school from summer vacation, I worried about what the other girls would think of me, if I'd fit in, how I looked to them, and what would be served for lunch. *Unlike* the first day back, my new cellie immediately asked me if I had any ice (aka meth) on me. I apologized and told her no, but that I wished I did. I hadn't tried amphetamines before, but this seemed as good of a place as any, and I would have made a fast friend.

Even without drugs, I learned the lay of the land and started talking to the other inmates. Like all relationships that start out of convenience and necessity, some were more superficial than others, some were based on the fact that we wanted to wear each other like puppets (aka fuck), and some because we were reading the same book. Like in real life.

It didn't take long for actual connections to be formed, excavated out of the stinking tar pit that was our lives. We'd talk for hours and hours and hours, day and night. And when we weren't talking, we were writing notes and drawing pictures to give to each other in the morning. It was like falling in love on, well, meth: accelerated and intense.

Though my ability to talk to anyone and everyone certainly helped, my popularity really skyrocketed late into my first week. From flimsy plastic chairs set up in rows, like toddlers in preschool, we watched bad prime-time TV. We shouted obnoxious catchphrases while watching that one show about the cool nerds, waiting for it to end so we could get to what we really wanted: the local evening news. It wasn't rare for these women to see someone they knew on the news. Every night, someone would purportedly have some "insider info" on what *actually* happened at that robbery, or who was snitching on whom. Anyway, there we were, chitchatting through the commercial break, when the too-familiar geographically ambiguous BREAKING NEWS music sliced through the din.

"In breaking news: internet sensation the *Hipster Grifter*, also known as Kari Ferrell, has been arrested in Philadelphia earlier this week."

Cue my most recent mug shot (not nearly as flattering as the first one) displayed on the screen. The pod hushed and watched the TV with rapt attention.

"Miss Ferrell, a young Asian woman from Salt Lake City, Utah, is being held on charges of felony forgery, identity fraud, and issuing bad checks. She first gained attention in the Williamsburg area of Brooklyn for writing lewd messages to men, whom she would later scam. She will be extradited to Utah and likely stand trial in the coming days."

The other anchor chuckled, "Hipster Grifter, ha, that's cute," before moving on to the next story.

Everyone stared at me, and my heart raced faster than Laura Bush through a stop sign. Then they erupted in cheers.

"Holy shit! You didn't tell us you were a celebrity!"

"You crazy bitch! You crazy biiiiiiiiitch!"

And then, "Is Utah in England?"

By the end of the second week I had found a groove. I wished that I could serve all of my time, however long it was going to be, in Philadelphia and was dreading going to Utah. This jail was fundamentally different; namely, it wasn't privately owned by Mormons. It also offered more autonomy. We were trusted to walk unaccompanied to the doctor, library, and commissary (where they sold little radios!) and were out of our cells the majority of the day. There was more to eat. I imagined that it was like living in a dorm of a twisted college experience I never had.

Recreation time was outside in the yard, a concrete pen with all the charm of a post–war era whorehouse. My newfound friends and I liked to spend our time there with our bodies pressed against the cool cement walls in the corner where the cameras couldn't see.

Twenty-four hours before the riot, we were sitting in the yard as Kelly worked her dexterous fingers through Char's voluminous afro with fast and precise movements, like the Liberace of box braids. Kelly's skills were famous, and the amount of *suckies* (hard candy) she charged for a styling reflected the demand. She had to work quickly, since touching another inmate was strictly against the rules. Of course, more salacious things took place on the regular, but there *is* a true intimacy to fondling someone's scalp, scaly and dry from paraben-only jail shampoo.

"Did you hear that bitch pussy-packed a whole gram of crack in?" Kelly asked Char.

"No wonder her lips be flappin' in the wind."

"Which pair?" I wondered aloud, desperate to make them laugh.

Kelly ignored me. "She's about to bring all of us down with her, including Officer Merkley."

I looked quizzically at Char, who responded with a scowl. "Officer Merkley casts a blind eye during after-visit searches if you make it worth her while, but I don't trust the bitch."

And with that, the conversation was over. I had learned that the information you were given was the information you were given and to ask for more was considered disrespectful.

Char's skepticism was justified not two hours later. There was a rat among us. Cells were being searched, books and drawings were sent flying through the air as guards (Officer Merkley included) turned bins upside down and violently shook out blankets. Inmates stood with their hands behind their backs, trying to look casual and unfazed, silently begging the guards to Step! Away! From the toilet paper! (There were lots of holes being stuffed on the regular, but the hollow part of the roll made for an excellent place to hide small pieces of contraband.)

In Spades's cell they found nothing besides a stash of perfume ads ripped out of magazines that had slipped through unnoticed by the mail sorters. Contraband of the most boring order. But when those flimsy samples were carelessly tossed into the trash, it set off an explosive chain reaction.

Spades protested as the officers walked out of their cell, barking at them to clean up the rest of their shit.

"My momma! They're taking my momma!" Spades wailed, eyes fixed on the plastic trash bag as it was carried away. We'd later find out that their stockpile consisted of only one scent, the perfume that Spades's momma, who had died the year before, had worn. Spades had been allowed a monitored release for four hours to say goodbye to the body that smelled nothing like what they remembered. When they made it back to the cell, I wondered why Spades didn't try pleading with the guards more, didn't try to explain *why* that perfume was so meaningful. Instead, they sat wondering why they hadn't pushed Officer Merkley—that two-timing snitch— over the fucking balcony railing when they had the chance.

The charges Spades had been arrested for were nonviolent. Maybe on the outs they'd go for a run or get some vitamin D from someone's son, but neither of those stress relievers were available here—it's easy to overthink things when you're stuck in a cage all day. We could do nothing as they slowly tiptoed to the edge of reason before taking the plunge into full-blown revenge.

Pressing our faces against the cell doors, our nightly ritual began. Words spat into the thin metal space. Voices competed to be heard. The guards could listen in if they wanted to, but we knew they were cozy in that high tower, scrolling through Craigslist casual encounters, droning on about lives that were only a little less boring than ours.

"What are you going to do?" one inmate asked. "We know you ain't gonna let this slide."

"You better make them come correct," another chimed in.

"Whatever you do, keep me out of it."

"Shut the fuck up, Tina! No one wants your musty vagina around anyway."

"So? What's the plan?"

"Just. Wait," Spades growled.

Despite the excitement of what was to come and the pod buzzing in anticipation, the moment I realized we weren't getting any additional details, my eyelids grew heavy. I welcomed this sensation with a sigh of relief, an exhalation of the breath I had been holding for the past several hours. My favorite part of the day was going to bed, because it was something the rest of the outside world was doing, too. A small semblance of normalcy.

That night, an all-too-familiar scene bounced around in my head. I dreamt about the people I scammed, their faces blurring together, dollar signs replacing their eyes. Watching from above as my body roamed through Union Pool, grabbing tips off the bar before they could make it into deserving hands. As I stuffed the loose bills into my BAM tote (swiped from some idiot whose philanthropy existed to serve his horniness for young women who liked "generous" lovers), my thumb rubbed against the personal inscription of the iPod I had hurriedly snatched off my roommate's nightstand earlier that day.

The stolen goods started to glow, pulsating illuminations like found weapons in a first-person shooter, each dollar growing brighter and brighter as the din of the bar quieted, the music stopped, and everyone turned in unison to stare at me, my eyes lit up by a disco ball, darting back and forth like one of those retro cat wall clocks on PCP. Panic started to swell, an orchestra of oboes in my chest, as I made a run for it.

I was almost out the door when a man swooped by, his fingers like a vise grip around my arm as we descended into darkness. Suddenly I was on a stage, hundreds of eyes staring through me, the words others had written blasting over the speakers.

"Inmate number 801725 is a wet, young Asiatic beaver from Salt Lake City. Subservient, ready to be fetishized, with a bizarre sexual proposition for every situation. White on the inside, yellow on the outside, this exotic little banana will make all of your manic pixie dreams come true. Bids start at $69."

I stuffed hundreds of blank checks into my mouth while the men around me clapped.

I woke up with a jolt, covered with sweat and wrapped in paper sheets. My stomach sank as I tried to dissect the dream before it floated away. Shame, fear, greed, pride (and the rest of the deadly sins), unspeakable loneliness, and most confusingly, a sense of gratification . . . that what? That I got what I deserved?

Morning light streamed in through the skylight and danced across my face. The rays should have been refreshing, but after waking from an imagined nightmare to face the reality of an actual one, they felt oppressive and claustrophobic.

An unnerving sense of serenity hung in the air of the dayroom, sitting empty even though the jail was at full capacity. This happened every few days after many of the girls hoarded enough Benadryl to knock them out for eighteen hours straight. I jumped at the opportunity to take a shower alone and rid myself of the night's trauma. Maybe I'd even get to have some alone time, a *ménage à moi*, if you will. There were plenty of people here who didn't give a fuck who was watching them give themselves a fuck, but I still needed my privacy.

I shuffled across the pod in my ill-fitting shower shoes that squeaked every time my heel kissed the ground, ensuring that I'd never be able to sneak up on a bitch.

"Yo, Kari, come here," I heard Spades shout-whisper.

I craned my neck around the corner into their cell.

"Got any eye drops I can trade for?"

"Nah, but my cellie does. I'm sure you can use them," I replied.

"I need the whole bottle."

"Okay, but if I broker this deal I get a tamale."

Ah, my first jailhouse demand. I felt like such an adult. My mouth watered as I thought about the culinary concoction made of smashed Fritos, Cheetos, and a Slim Jim.

"Deal. But remember, it's gotta be the whole bottle."

As is well-known, talking was always my specialty. I'd run circles around my victims, pepper in a few compliments, and the next thing they knew they'd be missing their wallets and their dignity. Turns out manipulating inmates is a lot harder than civilians, because my cellie wasn't having it.

"Nuh-uh. No way. Spades can kiss my ass."

My cellie loved to withhold, especially when it came to medical supplies.

"What if I said it was for me?" I fluttered my eyelashes.

"You look like you're having a stroke. And you can lick my ass."

Spades got ocular lube from someone else, and I never got my tamale. I pouted for a few hours, feeling stripped of the opportunity to prove myself useful, and therefore important. My ego knew no bounds, nor did my insatiable desire to feel high and mighty, even in the lowest of places. I was so fucking pathetic.

Back in the dayroom, we watched the minutes tick by until lockdown. Seated at the uncomfortable metal tables while playing cards, we told stories everyone had heard a hundred times in a hundred different ways (we were our own entertainment). Spades slowly padded over to our table in their homemade maxi pad slippers—pretty much exactly what it sounds like—face still wet with tears. They interrupted our game, voice manic and several octaves higher than normal.

"Watch this, y'all! I'm about to make shit wild up in here!" Spades's face contorted with every grief-fueled word.

Spades cautiously sidled up to the guards' station on the main floor, which looked like it came out of an underworld level in *Super Mario Brothers*: bricks stacked on top of one another, jutting out of the floor, creating a seven-foot-high barrier around two plain-looking elevated desks. Glancing at Officer Merkley as she made her rounds on the top tier, Spades stood on their tiptoes and stretched their body up as far as it could go, fishing for . . . what, exactly? Reeling their arm back to meet their body, fingers wrapped tightly around Merkley's tall silver coffee mug, they gave us a little "rah-rah" fist pump.

In one swift motion, Spades popped the lid off the mug and squirted eye drops into the drink before returning it to the desk. With a maniacal smile plastered on their face, they power-walked back to the table where we all sat in confused silence.

"Tetrahydrozoline," Spades laughed. "She'll be pissing out of her butthole for days."

"Tetra-what-the-fuck?"

"Hydro-zoline. My cousin went to school to be a pharmacist's assistant before she got caught buying crack at the YMCA. Told me all about it."

A flicker of a memory scratched at the back of my brain. Wrapped in a blanket on the floor of a roach-infested Bed-Stuy apartment, I hid from police who were combing the streets searching for my tattooed chest. An emotionless voice crackled out of the barely working radio in the corner, "A woman recently died at the Granville Price Chopper after her friends pranked her on

Halloween by spiking her drink with Visine. The active ingredi-
ent, tetrahydrozoline, is difficult to trace and . . ."

"Spades, that could kill her!" I hissed.

"Nah, baby, it would take more bottles than the commissary
has to do any of that shit."

I started to not-so-silently freak out, visions of dead cops in
my head, and even worse, headlines naming me as an accomplice.

"Jesus fucking Christ, Chee-na," Spades said. "Calm down or
you'll be the one laid out on the floor."

My panic was contagious, and the other girls started to demand Spades go and grab the mug, too. With a huff, Spades saun-
tered to the other side of the pod, making a show of taking their
sweet-ass time. As their fingers wrapped around the mug for a
second time, a porcine voice squealed from above.

"INMATE HARRIS, ON THE GROUND!"

Spades hesitated.

"NOW!"

Spades started to step away from the guard's station, at the
same time recoiling their arm, thrusting it out like a shot-putter,
launching the coffee mug at Officer Merkley. Their athletic prow-
ess left a lot to be desired and the mug fell short, exploding as it
made contact with the ground.

All of the air escaped my body with an "Oh, fuck," as the rest
of the pod erupted in cheers and whistles.

Things were escalating quickly. I felt lightheaded and my
thoughts raced. As panic took over my lizard brain, I wondered

if I would ever be able to inhale again. Was I going to die here? Images of my face turning blue like the guards' uniforms, limbs twitching erratically, flashed before my eyes. The last fleeting gasps of a desperate woman trying to do the right thing in all the wrong ways. An army of guards descended upon us, rushing down the stairs and yelling commands that were drowned out by the ear-piercing siren bouncing off the walls. In their haste, one of them tripped, causing all the others to fall like overweight, fleshy dominos.

As in times of war, the population quickly sorted into Us vs. Them, and we were united in the solidarity of being able to kick the enemy while they were (literally) down. Girls grabbed wildly at batons, pepper spray, whatever they could manage. Kelly emerged from the pile victorious, concealing something I couldn't see under her uniform—those damn quick hands, typically reserved for braiding, serving her in more nefarious ways. By this point I had pulled myself out of my stupor and was violently waving a lunch tray in front of my face. Out of the corner of my eye, I caught a flash of an inmate's jumpsuit walking away from the hot water dispenser. *Who was making ramen noodles at a time like this?*

Next thing I knew, a guard was clutching his face, screaming like a wounded animal. Striped Jumpsuit spun around, bowl in hand, scalding water dripping onto the floor, mixing with the coffee that was already there.

Shit *really* went bonkers after that. Guards had their tasers at the ready, fear and determination (but mostly fear) plastered across their faces, as they were pushed into a corner by inmates with everything and nothing to prove. Girls ran to their cells, not to retreat, but to grab heavier things to throw. Was that blood on the wall?

Spades swooped in next to me, my knight in overwashed, threadbare armor. "Let's go."

"You're not mad at me?" My insufferable need to be liked surfaced even in the midst of a goddamn riot.

"Nah, you were only trying to protect me."

And Officer Merkley, I thought.

"Don't worry, Chee-na," Spades said defiantly.

Soon after I made it to the safety of my cell, reinforcement barreled into the dayroom, guards whose faces were obscured by industrial-looking masks and actual firearms attached to their hips. They were screaming at everyone to get back into their cells, waving their batons and shields. That display was more than enough to halt the anarchic uprising, a sort of anticlimactic end to the most exciting thing that had happened to us in days.

After locking us down for forty-eight hours, the warden came to visit us in the pod. We were verbally reprimanded and told that any additional acts could add more time to our sentences. All things considered, we made it out mostly unscathed.

Kelly lost her library privileges for a month after she was caught with the flashlight she swiped off a guard so she could read at night.

Striped Jumpsuit was taken away and never seen again, but

I heard she was moved to federal prison and was much happier there. It was a common sentiment that prison was better than jail.

The guards never found out about the eye drops, but Spades was punished for trying to steal coffee and throwing a fit, and put in solitary confinement for ten days. News of their exploits reached the other pods, which led to an endless supply of snacks and cigarettes sent to their cell by sympathizers and fans.

As for me, I had for the first time in my life felt not like an "other," but part of a larger "them." The fact that this revelation came during a jail riot, and the "them" I was so desperate to be a part of were society's "others," is not lost on me. The riot led me to open my Chee-na eyes and see that at the end of the day, no one is good *or* bad. We're a confused mess of all the above, striving for the same thing: to hold the memory of our past lives close, as we trudge toward the unknown. Together.

Or at least until I was hauled off to Utah.

10

CON AIR

After the riot, the usual routine settled back in at the jail. Which is to say that for a few days afterward it all felt extra fucking dull.

The juxtaposition of the feelings you have while locked up is a total mindfuck. You sit there waiting like a sore on someone's ass while the most important thing in your life—your freedom— hangs in the balance. There is so little that you can control that it's better to save your energy and spare your mind the "what ifs," and accept the "normalcy" of your highly abnormal situation.

So, when something as momentous and crazy as a riot happens, the unpredictability of the real world briefly reenters your life, and it can feel like a time of mourning after it's gone again. For days, we fondly spoke about what happened, as if it had all transpired years ago. *Back in my day, we tried to poison the guards with OTC meds.* And, of course, like most stories passed around, again and again, from pod to pod, they started to take on their own form, metamorphosing into something grander and more ridiculous than the truth.

One afternoon I was sitting in a small chair outside of the infirmary, waiting to see the nurse practitioner (I was trying to get Klonopin for my anxiety . . . to trade for more chocolate). A young woman I hadn't seen before from another pod sidled up next to me.

"Holy shit, you're that girl on the news. What up? I'm Star."

I opened my mouth to respond when she cut me off.

"You were in that riot, huh? That shit be crazy, for real! I heard that when one of the officers fell they broke their arm and you could see the bone pop out. Did you see the bone pop out?"

"Uh . . ." I hesitated and looked at Star's deep brown eyes, wide with anticipation. "Yeah, I saw it . . . and I *heard* it, too—it was fucking disgusting!"

It would have been a disservice to *not* lie to her. I provided her with a little excitement to help her get through the day, *and* she'd be able to take that (mis)information back to her pod and feel like big queen shit for a minute. I was doing her a favor.

Star let out a whistle and shook her head in disbelief.

"Man, I wish I could have been there for that."

People like to joke that all jail does is make a better criminal. And based on my experiences, there's definitely a truth to that. When you're stuck in a vacuous void and there's nothing else to do, you talk. And you talk about what you know.

During a game of cards, it was laid out to me, in great detail, how to counterfeit money. From the printer I needed to buy, to where to get the right paper, to how long to soak the bills in brackish water to give them the perfect "wear and tear" of a circulated bill. One day I was passed a note from a woman who was an extremely skilled artist, cleverly nicknamed—wait for it—Art. I slowly unfolded the paper and revealed an intricately illustrated diagram on how to hot-wire a car, with a note scrawled at the top: *Just in case.*

But not all of our extracurriculars were so nefarious. Some were downright delightful. I learned how to origami a bath towel into a swan and elephant, like the kind of mementos that are left on your neatly made bed on a cruise ship. We used toothpaste to hang photos on the brick walls of our cells; memories of our kids, partners, and ourselves (everyone wanted you to know what they looked like in the real world.) The oil from the toothpaste would seep into the image, causing spots of swirled color to appear above a baby's smiling face, so it looked like he was about to be sucked into another dimension. I once made a bouquet of flowers out of discarded Reese's wrappers. We made do with what we had in order to make things feel a little more like home. I was like a law-breaking Martha Stewart. Oh, wait.

Upholding normalcy also meant that every morning we would use wet colored pencils to draw on eyeshadow and liner. We held our hair in place with "gel" that was made by soaking Jolly Ranchers in hot water and mixing it together with lotion. We maintained our brows by threading them with floss (imagine my surprise years later when I found out that threading was a method that has been used for thousands of years in Iran and India). We cherished our beauty routines and when they were disrupted, it sent some into a tailspin. For a time, I wondered why all of these women would go through the rigmarole of getting ready when they had nowhere to go and no one to impress. It soon became clear to me that they weren't doing it for anyone else. They were doing it for themselves.

I knew that my time in Philadelphia was coming to an end—I had been there for almost a month—but didn't know exactly when that was. I had heard that if I wasn't transferred within forty days I'd be released, so I was sort of holding out hope that might be the case. But what would I do if I was released? Go back to New York? Start a new life in some South American country? I needed to get back to Utah to make amends so that life could move forward, and I wished it would hurry up already. The road to redemption, I was learning, is paved with speed bumps and hurdles.

I slowly started to say goodbye to my fellow inmates, my friends, the people who had supported and helped me through the first leg of what I could only assume would be a long stint in the clink. We all made promises we knew we couldn't keep, like that we'd stay in contact or put money on each other's books—it's the thought that counts, after all.

Early one morning around 5:00 A.M., I was startled by a crackly voice coming through the intercom in our cell, breaking through the static: "Hollywood, let's go!"

My stomach churned as I grabbed my notebooks full of journal entries, drawings, and lists of real-world things I didn't want to forget (my favorite bands and movies). Those pieces of paper were the only thing I cared about, and I wasn't even sure I'd be able to keep them. The panic of the unknown swelled inside me. I hugged my cellie, thanked her for everything, and asked her to distribute my meager possessions—hair conditioner, shower shoes, colored pencils—as she saw fit, knowing damn well that she was going to keep them all.

A guard I had taken a liking to (he genuinely wanted the women under his care to succeed and had more than once written a letter of recommendation to a judge) unlocked the door and asked me to turn around so he could cuff me. I felt an incredible sadness and was scared shitless, the same feelings I had as a kid anytime we moved. Couldn't I stay here for another week?

As we exited the pod I unceremoniously yelled, "See you on the other side!" to the sleeping bodies of my compatriots, hoping they were being swaddled in pleasant dreams of a brighter future. I shuffled through the doors of what would turn out to be my preferred detention facility (akin to choosing your "favorite" Republican cabinet member to fuck) with my head held high.

We walked the long corridors of the labyrinthian building that was designed to be difficult for prisoners to remember to prevent escape, chains clanking with every step. The guard asked me if I had plans when I got out. I told him about my dreams of becoming a writer, of telling stories, of trying to make something real and tangible out of my life. Of not letting *this* be my legacy. He sincerely wished me the best of luck and dropped me off at a holding cell, removing my cuffs and letting the door slam behind him as he walked away. Something I could only dream of doing at that moment.

A few moments later another officer stopped by and threw a large plastic bag at me. Inside were the clothes I was wearing when I got arrested and a hair tie. I welled up a bit as I changed out of my jail uniform and slid my boobs into a real bra and my legs into soft denim. The dam broke and tears spilled over as I slipped the elastic band around my wrist. Oh, to think that there was a time when this was the tightest thing around this part of my body.

As I sat alone in the cell with my feelings for hours, waiting for whatever was to come, I cycled through my usual list of worries: *What was going to happen to me? Would I go to prison? Would I ever have real friends again? Would I ever be able to make it up to people? Would I get better?* Sitting firmly at the top of that list, somewhat embarrassingly, was *When would I get the rest of my stuff back?*

When I was arrested after getting off the bus in Philly, my gigantic suitcase was put in the trunk of the squad car, but after that I lost sight of it. All of my worldly possessions were being held together by a flimsy zipper in a storage locker that was who knows where. It stressed me the fuck out and actually hurt my heart to think about my favorite sweater being unworn, lifeless without a body to fill it. It may seem ridiculous to have such deep feelings for a cheap garment, especially when you're on a most wanted list and facing a trial and you haven't talked to your family in months, but this is what imprisonment does to your brain. This is what you're reduced to.

I was attempting to mentally catalog all of my things (had I grabbed my favorite pen off the counter back in Bed-Stuy?) when I was interrupted by the all-too-familiar buzz of a door unlocking. Two people in civilian clothing (one male and one female) walked toward me.

"Ferrell! Right before our very eyes, as I live and breathe," the stocky man declared.

"You ready to journey back west, outlaw?" the barely five-foot woman asked.

"Yee-fucking-haw." I stood up with a tip of my invisible cowboy hat.

"They said you were funny. I'm Detective Penfield, this is Detective Young. We'll be your entourage for the duration of the trip. Let's go," the male detective said.

I don't know whom I was expecting to pick me up, but it wasn't these two. They were so . . . nonthreatening. Nice, almost. Was this exciting for them? Had they done this before? I had questions, but bit my tongue. There would be plenty of time to ask.

"Here, put this on," Penfield instructed as he tossed a light-weight windbreaker that looked straight out of the early '90s toward me. The bright blues and neon pinks were a pleasant contrast to the banal color scheme that had ruled my life for the last month.

"There's a hole in each of the pockets so you can keep your hands in them and no one will know you're cuffed. We don't want to frighten your fellow passengers," Detective Young explained.

"Fellow passengers?" I asked.

Up until this point I had been given zero information about my transport. I hadn't known if we were driving cross-country or if I was going to be shoved into a cattle car on a freight train. If we were to fly, I assumed it would be like the 1997 cinematic masterpiece that is *Con Air* and I would be convict Cameron Poe (expertly portrayed by Nicolas Cage), naturally.

Detective Young explained that I wouldn't be strapped in with John Malkovich or any other prisoners; that I'd actually be boarding a commercial flight with families and old people and snacks. Wait, would I be getting snacks?

I slipped the jacket over my head and shoved my hands into the pockets until they touched in the middle, then glanced at my reflection in the windowpane and winced. The windbreaker was massive. I looked like a wannabe hip-hop dancer double amputee . . . but not like a prisoner, so there was that.

"Alright, let's do this," I said, as if I were the one calling the shots.

Detective Young pointed at my hands, and I instinctively

held my wrists out so he could fasten my government-distributed stainless-steel bracelets.

"You shouldn't have," I quipped as they tightened around me.

We piled into a Philly cruiser, chauffeured by a random officer who acted as if it was a great sacrifice to leave the jail and drive us to the airport. Detective Young sat up front while Penfield sat in the back with me. I watched our heads bob in unison as we drove over bumps and potholes, thinking about how bizarre it was that we were all humans who had bodies that were relatively the same, but were leading such different lives. A stoner thought without the stones.

The car ride was too quick, over before I even knew it. Soon, I would be looking down at the landscape we'd whizzed by, passing over millions of people who weren't being flanked by two stewards of the law. People who had never had to eat ramen noodles made with lukewarm water because their hot water privileges had been revoked after a riot.

We pulled up to the curb of the airport, taking up space typically reserved for people to bid their loved ones adieu. The driver waved unceremoniously as he started to pull away.

"Wait!" I yelled. "What about my suitcase?"

"You'll have to work that out with the jail," he said. "Someone will need to come and pick it up—we won't hold it for more than thirty days." And with that he sped off.

With a lump in my throat I told myself to buck up. Hold it together. Get through this flight. Get through this life.

As an unlikely trio, we navigated through the airport. I wondered how we looked to other people shuffling toward the TSA, two straight-laced white folks guiding an Asian girl around by the elbow. It wasn't lost on me that I had acted out this exact scenario dozens of times with my own family.

At security I was told that I didn't need to take my shoes off, but would need to be searched. As the agent ran her hands over me, I knew that *she* knew that I was a prisoner, but to her credit she didn't say or do anything that would give that away. I appreciated that morsel of kindness and hoped all my other interactions of the day would follow suit.

We were walking toward the gate when Detective Penfield said he was going to go to the Hudson News to grab a Coke.

"Do you want anything?"

"No, all good," Young replied.

"Ferrell?"

I was caught off guard. It felt like ages since someone had asked me what I wanted. Was this a trick?

"Umm, I'll take a Coke, too," I said quickly. "And some Starbursts!"

I was in no position to press my luck, but who fucking cares when you don't have any luck to lose.

"You got it," he said.

"He must really like you," Detective Young said as Penfield walked away.

"I've been told I'm very likable . . . for better or worse."

"Yeah, well, your charm is undeniable. I can see why all those boys fell for you. But you don't fool me, not for one second."

"Good thing I'm not trying to fool anyone right now. Besides, that's rich coming from someone who was bamboozled into working a thankless job for little over minimum wage."

She raised her thin eyebrows in surprise.

"I've also been told that I'm very intuitive," I said, smirking.

Detective Penfield returned with a bag and sat down next to us. He opened a bottle of soda with a *kshhh* and took three large swigs.

"Ahh, nothing more refreshing than an ice-cold Coca-Cola. You know?"

I stared at him, trying not to let him see how disappointed I was that I myself wasn't riding the invigorating caustic wave of corn syrup and empty calories.

"Don't worry, I didn't forget about you, Ferrell. But you're going to have to wait until we're on the plane, due to your . . . situation." He nodded toward my suffocated and sweaty hands still stuffed into the kangaroo pouch pocket of the jacket.

I thanked him with a smile and then turned toward Detective Young.

"I have to pee."

She rolled her eyes and sighed, "Alright, get up. Let's go."

We walked into the bathroom, which was thankfully mostly empty.

"So, uh, how does this work?" I asked.

"I can't uncuff you. I'll unbutton and unzip you, but you're going to have to do the rest as best you can. Try not to make a mess."

She lifted the jacket up, exposing my midriff as she tugged at my pants. I almost made another "You're not even going to buy me dinner first?" joke, but thought better of it and kept my mouth zipped as my jeans were being undone.

A woman came in and eyed us as she walked briskly toward a vacant stall. I considered shrieking or drooling in hopes she would think I was experiencing some kind of medical emergency, but by the time I could produce enough spit she was already making love to the toilet (the noises coming from that end of the restroom were impressive in their ferocity).

"For the love of God, make it quick," Young commanded.

I walked into the stall and shut the door, locking it with both hands, and shimmied my pants and underwear down to my ankles and hovered. *What are you doing?* I thought to myself. *Who knows when the next time you're going to be able to piss in private is. Get comfortable.* I planted myself down and looked at Detective Young's feet right outside of the stall, standing guard.

What a luxury this was. I promised myself that once I was a free woman I'd never take private urination for granted. I finished up without too much difficulty and opened the door, presenting myself to Detective Young with a *ta-da*.

When we got back to the gate everyone was standing in that funny faux-urgent, anticipatory way that people do when they're about to get on a plane. A mad dash to sit for an extended period of time.

"We are now going to begin boarding for Flight 2103 to Salt Lake City. For those needing extra time or assistance, we welcome you to do so now," a gate agent said cheerily over the intercom.

Detective Penfield motioned toward me and we walked past the horde of passengers waiting impatiently for their turn. I felt everyone's eyes bore holes through me. This was pre–*Game of Thrones* but it very much felt like the infamous scene of Cersei Lannister being paraded through the town, the Maester following behind ringing the bell. Except that instead of being naked I was wearing a stupid fucking oversized windbreaker. *Shame, shame, shame.* Did they know that I was handcuffed under that nylon tent? Unlikely. But I knew, and that's what mattered. That's what has always mattered.

The flight attendant at the head of the plane gave a knowing nod to the detectives and wouldn't look me in the eye. We walked to the very back, the final row, the one that everyone stands next to while they wait to pee. We clumsily plopped into our seats. I was in the middle, squished between two people whose sole job was to get me across state lines in one piece. We buckled our seat belts and waited for our ascension into the mysterious beyond.

As we took off, I noticed Detective Penfield gripping the armrests, knuckles turning white.

"Nervous?" I asked.

"I hate flying," he grumbled, closing his eyes tight.

"What kind of God would take a plane down that has a convict aboard before they get their Coca-Cola?"

"Not. Comforting," Penfield said through gritted teeth.

When we reached the required altitude to lean our seats back (though ours didn't because of the aforementioned bathroom) and lower our tray tables, Penfield retrieved the Hudson News treasure sack out from underneath the seat in front of him.

"Your hands must remain cuffed and concealed," he instructed.

Wait, so this *was* a trick.

He pulled the soda out, twisted the cap off, and held it up to my lips. I took gulps like someone who was drowning and coming up for air. It was *everything*. The chemical-y taste that only a Coca-Cola could provide sent me into a state of sugar-induced euphoria. The liquid burned my throat as it went down and I relished the pain. I didn't even care that it was lukewarm at this point. It was heaven.

I nodded and he lowered the bottle.

"Thank you," I said with all the seriousness of someone who had just been dragged out of the water by a guardian angel.

As we cruised through the air in a hunk of metal at five hundred miles per hour and with nothing else to do, I tried to get to know the detectives. I asked them about the job, if it was what they expected, if they acknowledged the pitfalls of the system, what the toughest case they'd ever worked on was.

They were as honest as they could be. The job was hard, tiresome, and mostly monotonous. Assisting in a cross-country extradition was rare (a first for both of them), and they could usually be found sitting at their desks for ten-plus hours a day. They agreed that the institution of incarceration wasn't perfect, but felt strongly that it was necessary. We debated back and forth on this a bit and eventually agreed to disagree.

We talked at length about how I wasn't the "typical criminal," and I pushed back on what that even meant. Their response was tinged with racism in the way that only a white person can project, steadfast in the belief that they weren't racist at all, not one bit. We also discussed the hubbub that surrounded my case, and they revealed that they were surprised that the state cared so much about imprisoning someone who had committed a relatively low-stakes and common crime. They agreed that it was intense and crazy how my story had taken off and spread like a virus. Detective Young expressed that she understood why: that it was because everyone was trying to wrap their heads around how someone who looked so innocent could do something so naughty.

They listened patiently as I explained the model minority myth, and how it served as a tool to drive a wedge between Asians and other non-white people, ultimately succeeding in ensuring that the conservative white agenda was withheld. Detective Penfield balked and told me that that wasn't the way he saw it at all, as he unwrapped each individual Starburst and popped it into my mouth.

Suddenly, the flight attendant's voice boomed over the intercom, letting us know that we were about to descend into the promised land. Again, Penfield gripped the armrests as if that would do jack shit if anything catastrophic were to actually happen. But I got it. I understood the need to tell yourself whatever you had to to calm your nerves and face your fears. As we made our way closer to the ground, I shifted my body so that my cuffed hands could grip my own armrest through the jacket.

The wheels kissed the tarmac with a jolt. We had made it to the city of salt in one piece. Some of the passengers clapped, and I imagined it was for me. After all, the prodigal daughter had returned. And wasn't that deserving of some applause?

11

THE LONG HAUL

When I left Utah to move to New York, I never expected to return. As we made our way from Salt Lake City International Airport to my new home (jail #2), I watched the snow-capped mountains pass by through the tinted windows of the transport van. They were so large and sure of their existence, firm and unmoving as we sped down the highway. I tried to take strength from them, but I was defeated. I'd arrived with my tail tucked between my legs, back to beg for forgiveness.

We pulled into the entrance of the jail—the same one I'd been booked at before—and I lifted myself out of the van to say my goodbyes to Detective Penfield and Detective Young. I quipped that I hoped it had been as good for them as it was for me, and Penfield wished me the best of luck.

I went through a handful of processes that I was, unfortunately, becoming used to. I shed my street clothes, exchanging them for a uniform, and got my asshole examined. I waited in a holding pod while they decided where to put me. And then I was questioned by two detectives, different from the ones who escorted me from Philadelphia.

"State your full name," one demanded.

"Kari Michelle Ferrell."

"State your date of birth."

"February 26, 1987," I responded, glancing toward the camera in the corner, propped up on a tripod with its wide-lensed mouth and blinking red eye.

"State of birth?"

"I was actually born in South Korea. Seoul."

The detective frowned, as if I had personally offended him by daring to be born outside of this great country, the one he most assuredly felt he was protecting.

"When did you immigrate to the United States?" he questioned sternly.

Immigrate? I had never been asked this before. Had I immigrated here? Was I an immigrant? Not that there was anything wrong with being one, of course. Maybe I was more of a stranger in my own land than I thought. Is adoption actually immigration? What if—

"Ferrell!"

"Uh, sorry?" I shook my head and came out of my foreigner's fog.

"I repeat: When did you immigrate to the United States?"

"Well, I was adopted as a baby. I came to the US when I was five months old. So," I continued while counting on my fingers, "July 1987. I'm a citizen."

"So you obtained US citizenship in July of 1987?"

"I think so? I don't know the exact date that I got my citizenship, but we went to court on July thirty-first . . . my 'celebration day.' That's what my family calls it."

The detective who had been silent up until this point coughed as he scribbled a note on the file sitting on the cold metal table before him.

"Do you affirm that you are in the United States legally?"

"Yes, absolutely," I replied.

Silent detective jotted down another note.

"Okay, those are all the questions we have . . . for now."

The two detectives got up and walked out, *ICE* printed in large, bold yellow letters on the back of their jackets. At the time I didn't know what that acronym stood for. I only knew—and palpably felt—that those two gentlemen seemed to resent my being here. Not in jail, but in the country.

It was freezing in the small room and I shivered, wondering if the ICE detectives were an interrogation tactic or if I was being a pussy. After what could have been fifteen or fifty minutes, two different officers walked in. They were in plain clothes, but I knew they were also detectives by the way they held their heads, like a stick was inserted up their ass, the rod traveling all the way up their spineless backs.

"Ferrell, we have a few more questions for you. Thanks for your patience."

I laughed. "As if I have some kind of choice? Ask away."

In retrospect, I gave them way too much information. I thought that if I "complied" I would look favorable to the judge, jury, and executioner and they'd take pity on me. I thought I was helping me help myself. After spilling most of the beans on how I fucked up, how sorry I was, and how I felt knowing that I was a disappointment to everyone, the detectives asked if I wanted a lawyer.

"Oh, god dammit," I whispered through gritted teeth, knowing that I had fucked up yet again.

Around midnight, a guard finally took me to the pod that I would call my home for the next several months. As I walked in I saw startled heads pop up one by one, awakened by the reverberation of the heavy door closing behind me.

"Holy shit," I heard someone squeal. "It's Kari *motherfucking* Ferrell!"

I looked around, not knowing where the greeting came from. Out of the corner of my eye I saw someone waving frantically. I squinted, willing my eyeballs to zoom in, but without my contacts I was shit out of luck. I waved back, hoping it was a friend but taking my chances on it being an enemy.

I entered the cell I was instructed to go to and slid the door shut with a loud and satisfying (to the guards) click. A putrid odor immediately hit my nostrils. I retched, looking around in disgust, and finally found the source of the smell curled up on the floor, head resting against the stainless steel toilet-sink.

"Jesus, it smells like the Hindenburg disaster in here," I said. "Are you okay?"

I got a groan in response. Shrugging, I threw a sheet over my shitty mattress and fell face down onto it. I rolled up my towel and tucked it underneath my head. I breathed through my mouth, trying to block out the stench. I had to pee, but I willed my bladder to hold for a few more hours as I wistfully fell asleep.

The next morning I woke up from a dream that I pissed my pants in the line for the DMV. Panicking, I patted the area around me, happy to discover that it was dry to the touch. I stood up and stared at the young woman passed out in the same place and position I'd found her in hours before.

I lightly poked her shoulder. Nothing. I poked it a little harder. Still nothing. I sighed and grabbed her firmly and shook her.

"GET THE FUCK AWAY FROM ME!" she shrieked. "Who the fuck do you think you—"

She looked gray as she turned toward the toilet and vomited into it. The sour smell of whatever it was she was expelling filled the room again.

"Sorry, I . . . I don't feel good," she explained miserably.

"Yeah, I can see that, and I'm so sorry, but I have to pee."

She somehow gathered herself into a standing position, and

pressed the button on the toilet. There was an eardrum-shattering *WOOSH* as all of the excrement in the bowl was sucked down into the sewer with violent force.

I sat down and looked straight out into the pod. There was no privacy here. Everyone could see everything. Incarceration is designed to be that way. Carnal and archaic.

"I'm Madyson, by the way."

"I'm Kari. Are you . . . okay?"

"Heroin," she replied. No more explanation needed.

Madyson looked at me with sad eyes as she continued to vomit. I wet a washcloth and wiped around her mouth and hugged her.

Over the next few days, Madyson sobered up enough to tell me she was in jail for drug-related theft charges. She had a mentally unstable mom and a younger sister that she took care of. There had been several arrests over the past few years, but her judge must have been—as we inmates often remarked—fucked good the night before, because she always got time served and community service. Until now.

The problem was that Madyson, despite her best efforts, couldn't stay away from smack. She did her best and lamented to me that she didn't understand why her son wasn't enough to keep her away from the shit. She also said that being locked up was the only time she ever felt like herself, because it was the only time she wasn't shooting up. My heart broke for her.

Fortunately, she had a pretty supportive family. They didn't know how to tell her they still loved her, so they put money on her books instead. She graciously shared her candy and ramen noodles with me until my mom, a fan, or a journalist sent some money my way. Beyond being generous, Madyson was as smart as a whip (when her brain was able to function properly). She wasn't the first to prove to me that anyone and everyone can end up behind bars, but she certainly was the one to hammer that point home.

Madyson patiently explained the lay of the land to me and what everyone was doing there (both the stories they told and the one she claimed was real). She was my guiding light through a lot of troubled times, and I hoped to offer the same to her.

I later found out that the person who had shouted my name in the middle of the night when I came into the pod was Haylee Taylor, a girl I had gone to high school with. She was part of the popular crowd, a cheerleader, and her mom had been one of my Girl Scout troop leaders. She was snotty and stuck-up and knew that her worth as a white Mormon twat in Utah was greater than mine. But here we were now, together. Free from the confines of a real-world hierarchy, we were on a level playing ground.

When we were released from our cells the next morning I slowly walked up to where she was sitting on a metal stool, reading a letter that looked like it had been read a million times.

"Haylee, wow, what are you doing here?" I asked.

She looked up and gave me a toothy smile that a sudden sadness wiped off her face.

"Do you remember Chris Bawden?" she asked.

I hadn't heard his name in forever. "Yeah, I used to skip class and steal dog food from Walmart with him. How is he these days?"

"He's good. I mean, he's dead. But he *was* good . . . before the dying or whatever," she responded.

"Holy shit, what happened?" I asked, feeling the loss of a friend I hadn't spoken to for a decade.

"OD'd a couple of years ago. He's the one who got me into this shit," Haylee said with tears welling up in her eyes. She whispered, "I miss him so fucking much."

"I'm so sorry, Haylee. That all of this happened." I went to hug her.

"Ferrell, no physical contact!" the guard on duty warned.

"Thanks, yeah, I mean it's okay. I mean, I'm not okay, but yeah. I think I'll name this one after him." She gently rubbed her belly.

"You're pregnant?" I asked in a tone I immediately regretted. "I mean, congratulations! When are you due?"

"I only took a positive pee test a couple of days ago. I get my first ultrasound next week, but I think I'm about two months in."

"Do you . . . think you'll be out when . . ." I stopped before I could finish the question.

"I fucking better be," Haylee replied with confidence.

Haylee was one of *many* who were pregnant in the adult detention center, and one of three in our pod. As bad as my situation was, they were a reminder that it could always be worse. It should come as no surprise that jails and prisons are not designed for women, which is glaringly obvious in many ways, but especially so when it comes to healthcare. There is a lack of access to everything from mental health resources to menstrual products. And when you consider that, statistically, many women who enter the system have histories of sexual abuse and trauma, how can one be surprised that sticking them in a cage where men can watch them take a shit isn't a reformative experience?

And for pregnant women, it's an even more stressful and dehumanizing situation. From poor nutrition to inconsistent sleep schedules to lack of prenatal care and support, they bear the brunt of a structure designed to terrorize the soul. When expecting mothers do get medical treatment, they have virtually no autonomy or control over their care, and are often shackled—even when they give birth. After the baby is delivered, mothers are typically allotted only twenty-four hours with their newborn.

I was surrounded by mothers, grandmothers, sisters, and wives (and some sister-wives), who were undoubtedly the strongest people I've ever known. The universe dealt them blow after blow and they were still fucking standing.

The next morning I had a court appearance, which meant waking up at the ass crack of dawn to shuffle aboard a prison transport bus that would take us to the courthouse downtown. I always liked the bus rides because they were my only opportunity to see the outside world. We didn't have windows in our cells, so the sight of a gas station or grocery store was enough to get my juices flowing. It was also the only time we got to talk to the male inmates. Though most of them were not my type, it felt good to be desired—even when that desire was expressed through vulgar catcalls and kissy noises.

Once we arrived, we drove into a secret underground parking garage, ensuring that the public would be spared the icky sight of us, and were put into holding cells with years of history etched into the walls by prisoners past.

I <3 Shirley my baby!

Praying 4 every1 here 2day

FUCK JUDGE KOCH AND FUCK THAT BITCH DANIELA HERNANDEZ

I doubted that anyone was praying for me, but said one of my own to a God I no longer believed in, just in case.

Dear Heavenly Father, please bless this day and let me get time served and released. I promise to be a better person from this day forward. Like, for real this time. In the name of your son, Jesus Christ, amen.

That was the day I realized that God was dead. Not because I didn't get out (though that wasn't helping His case), but because I watched as Women of Color received harsher sentences than white people who had committed the exact same crimes. I saw a young mother sentenced to twenty-five years with no chance for parole for selling cocaine so she could afford formula. She sobbed into her sack lunch, crying her son's name and cursing the father's, as we all tried to comfort her but didn't know what to say. I heard officers say "see ya next time" to women upon their release, not letting them leave such a cursed place with a smidge of dignity.

From that day forward, I may not have instantly become a better person, but I certainly became a more determined one. My prayers were no longer said to some magical, invisible man. Instead they were directed toward Madyson, Haylee, Maria, Rosa, Nikki, and all the other countless women who held me up (sometimes after holding me down). These very overlooked, very real mothers, grandmothers, sisters, and wives were the ones worthy of praise. They were my grace and my support. They were my salvation.

12

THE LONG HAUL PART 2

ELECTRIC CHAIR BOOGALOO

Five months and countless court appearances later, I was still behind bars and had no idea what my sentence would be. Predictably, I wasn't the same person who had walked through the doors nearly half a year before. Not that I believed I'd receive a life sentence, but I had started to think that I could live in jail forever, that maybe it wasn't *so* bad. I realized I could lie to myself as easily as I could to other people.

There's an odd, ironic sense of liberation that comes with doing time. Say bye-bye to many of your adult responsibilities. I no longer had to worry about rent, or bills, or how I was going to get my next meal. The firm grip that capitalism had on me was loosened by sheer lack of choice, which honestly felt refreshing.

I hadn't realized how much of my time in the real world was oc-
cupied by trying to make a decision. When they're all made for
you, you get to ease up a little bit. At the same time, I wistfully
reminisced about the days when I was barely scraping by (all of
them), when the world's unpredictability felt like a welcome challenge I could overcome (with felonious activities). I wondered if
how I lived before was a better or worse situation than the one I
had found myself in.

But even if my "real world" had changed, the actual real world
for many others had not. Life kept on moving, as broken and
beautiful as ever. Milestones were met by children who could only
see their mothers once a week through layers of plexiglass. Evic-
tion notices were posted to front doors where the breadwinner
was behind bars. Like in the movies, gang alliances were made
and broken, affecting not only those on the inside but also those
on the outside.

The business acumen of many of these women was downright
impressive and rivaled that of the most successful and cunning
of Fortune 500 CEOs. I once asked someone why they hadn't
gone to business school, and their response was to ask me how
many drugs they'd have to sell to afford that. I knew that as bad
as I felt I had it, I was privileged and so very lucky throughout my
life—so lucky that I hadn't thought about how impossible it is to
pull yourself up by the bootstraps when you're shuffling around
in dollar store flip-flops because you can't afford boots in the first
place.

*   *   *

Once I was settled in, I started to receive what I lovingly referred to as *fan mail*—you know, to keep my ego inflated. Realistically, they were letters from random strangers that ran the gamut as to why they felt compelled to correspond with a convict. There was a guy who felt it was his calling to get me to accept our Lord and Savior (been there, done that), a woman who applauded my actions and wanted to know how she could get into my line of work, and one person of anonymous gender who took fetishization to the next level. I wrote back to every single person, in hopes that they'd want to continue communicating with me—even if it was about how they wanted to hogtie me and feed me kimchi until I exploded. It was a better alternative than focusing on how many times my roommate had to flush the toilet when making her third deposit of the day, thanks to the slop we ate.

I also received mail from several news outlets. Most wanted quick answers to questions that would only set me up to look foolish. *Did you know that what you were doing was wrong? Why did you need the money? What is a hipster anyway?* I chose to respond to most of these inquiries with a letter of my own that simply stated "No comment," spending hours decorating the envelopes with scenes of cute monsters floating above a dark city of high-rises.

One day during mail call, the guard shouted my last name— always a good feeling, someone was thinking of me!—and handed me a large manilla envelope. My elation disappeared. Nothing good

comes out of a large envelope with no return address. I carried it
gingerly back to my cell, as if it were a bomb that could detonate
at any moment. I plopped myself down on my cot as the mattress
made its usual loud, sad, trombone fart noise. I pinched the metal
clasp together forcefully (like the legs of the town prude), and peeled
the paper away from its gummy glue (like the town slut). Inside was
exactly one piece of paper printed on letterhead with a bold logo on
the top left. It must have gotten wet in transit, because it took me a
second to decipher what it said: a bloody red *Inside Edition*.

I, of course, had heard of the program and recalled catching
random episodes when I was younger, when I didn't fully understand the fairly exploitative nature of the stories (probably because
the entirety of the '90s could be considered "fairly exploitative").
The gears in my head started turning, and before I even read the
words on the page I was thinking about how this could be great
exposure for me. How, exactly? I didn't know, but much of my time
was spent grappling with the fact that I might get out of jail and
have to be a *Kevin Federline type*: living off the infamy, collecting
pennies to make club appearances, trying to make my name as a
wrestler (yeah, he did that).

The letter was from a producer named Lizzie Foster who said
that they understood the intricacies of my situation and wanted to
give me an opportunity to explain my side. She wrote that she had
reached out to some of my friends and acquaintances (aka, victims) who were willing to talk. I didn't like the way that sounded,
but I pushed it out of my brain.

The next day, when we were released from our cages into the dayroom, I held the envelope. This time instead of like a bomb, I treated it like the goddamned Hope Diamond, making sure its sparkle and gleam was seen by all.

"Well, it's happened," I said as I sat at a table where Nikki was.

"Oh, yeah? What's that?" she asked without much interest.

I was annoyed by the lack of enthusiasm for me and my situation. Maybe it was because this was not the first time I had bragged like this, nor would it be the last. I boasted a lot when I was lying, but I boasted even more when I didn't have to lie.

"I'm going Hollywood, baby!"

Despite her apathy, I traded Nikki some ramen noodles, a Snickers bar, and slightly used ChapStick for a single five-minute call. Honestly, a fair bargain.

I stood at one of the four pay phones bolted to the brick wall, trying to listen to the voice coming through the earpiece.

"Kari, can you hear me?" Lizzie asked.

I pleaded with my fellow inmate callers beside me. "Can you guys tone it the fuck down for a second?" And then I said into the receiver, "Yeah, sorry about that. I'd like to participate in your interview."

"Oh, great! I was hoping you'd say yes. I'll send you a packet shortly of what we're thinking and some history on the program."

"Okay, cool. I'm interested in talking not only about myself but some of the things I've experienced and seen while incarcerated," I explained. I imagined Lizzie on the other end, sitting in her fancy midtown office, taken by my professionalism. I bet she hadn't worked with a convict like me before.

"Well, we'll have to see what the other producers say, but that could probably fit into our piece. I'll say that people, our viewers, are really, really interested in *you*," Lizzie said.

We were interrupted by the omniscient robot voice alerting us that we only had sixty seconds left. I hung up after the call was over and walked back to my cell, my mind racing with the possibilities. Maybe all wouldn't be lost. I could pull myself out of this; I could surpass Kevin Federline.

I daydreamed about a camera crew coming to the jail, the warden granting an exception to the rule and allowing me to wear an emerald green ball gown that sparkled under the fluorescent lights as I descended one of the staircases. I shook my head, dismayed that even my fantasies had become imprisoned. The thought dissipated as the crackly voice of Officer Shoals came over the intercom.

"Ferrell, ever heard this one?"

I listened intently as note by note music started to fill the barren cell, crescendos cutting through the space of nothingness and vibrating through our souls.

"What the fuck is this racket?" Madyson shouted, her voice getting lost in the screams of the song.

"It's Refused and the song is 'New Noise,'" I declared.

"Ding, ding, ding!" Officer Shoals mimicked the sound of a game show's winning bell. "That's six in a row, a new record."

I don't remember how it happened exactly, but Shoals and I had developed a friendship of sorts. For all intents and purposes we were coworkers: he was getting paid for his job and I was paying for mine. One day we started talking about music and discovered that we had similar tastes, and from that night on Shoals and I would play a captive game of Name That Tune. Nothing salacious ever happened between the two of us, despite what some of the other inmates thought (not that I didn't fantasize about it), but we both benefited by having someone to talk to about common interests. After all, it wasn't only the inmates who were trapped there.

After my story had originally broken, while I was in hiding in Brooklyn, I began a correspondence with the editor in chief of a culture website called Animal New York. It was reminiscent of what *VICE* used to be (the founder won't be too pleased with this comparison, but it's true), a combination of actual news with a focus on street art and New York City politics. People have asked why, out of all the publications who were vying for interviews, I chose Animal. The answer was simple: they were the only ones who didn't stink of desperation and promised me an uncensored platform. There were rumors that Nick Denton, the founder of Gawker Media, was seen pounding his fists on the conference table during an all-hands meeting, yelling about how ridiculous it was that they couldn't secure an exclusive with me.

Whatever the case, while I was incarcerated I wrote letters to

Animal, which they'd scan and post and rack up views. I wrote about my experiences with the grace of a shock jock radio DJ and responded to tweets that Animal printed and mailed, weeks old by the time they got to me. Mail is the main way inmates stay connected to the world and their people. But unlike most inmates, it was also my platform.

One day I sat hunched over the small metal table in my cell, scrawling notes on a yellow legal pad—bullet points of the things I wanted to make sure I mentioned in my next letters, and during the interview with *Inside Edition*. I hated seeing myself as a product, something to be displayed and fondled (arguably what I had been running from my entire life), but I knew that there was a right and wrong way to tell my story. My story. *My* story. If it was a tragedy or a comedy, I wasn't sure, but I knew that it was mine.

"Psst!"

I whipped my head around to see Jenn #3 (not Jenn #1, who hit her ex with a hairbrush and got an aggravated assault charge and not Jenn #2, who tried to eat a bag of cocaine when she was pulled over on the highway and was handcuffed looking like she had hoovered a bag of powdered donuts) gesturing wildly as if she were trying to reel in a fish.

"What's up?" I asked, trailing Jenn #3 into the shower room. I shifted from side to side nervously. If we got caught in here it would be an automatic week in the hole.

"A'ight, listen," she said. "I'm taking Jenn [#2] on a date tonight. Making her a Frito pie, a dozen roses, the whole shebang."

"That's sweet, and then what? A nice walk through the park?"

"Ah, you know what—fuck you. To think I was going to give you a full phone card, too."

My ears perked up. That was no small bargaining chip.

I took the bait. "What do you need me to do?"

"So after our date, I wanna take things to the next level."

Much like being in high school with a new lover, there were logistics in jail. There were rules that required evasion. You had to sneak around to get what you wanted.

"And you want me to be your third? Get to the point."

"I need you to keep the guards away from her cell. That's where it's going to go down, if you know what I mean. Officer Garza lets us hang towels for added privacy when we're taking a shit. I need ten minutes."

"That's it?" I asked a little too quickly.

"I only *need* five minutes, because this tongue be magic, but I'm adding a buffer in case."

I thought about the phone card and how many people I could reach out to who didn't want to hear from me.

"Okay, I'll do it."

That night I watched Jenn and Jenn gaze into each other's eyes, pure elation and adoration when the origami flowers were presented in a plastic cup. I saw Jenn search for me, and I nodded dutifully from a nearby table, as they disappeared behind the precariously placed towel.

I smiled to myself, happy that someone was getting their

whistle wet even though I wished it could have been me. It had been a long time since I had a hot dog thrown down my hallway and longer still since it had happened organically and not as a manipulation tactic. As I was counting the exact amount of months it had been, I noticed Officer Garza making his way past the cells on the top tier. What the fuck? Garza was the laziest CO we had and he often skipped doing rounds altogether. And not only was he doing them, but he was doing them fast, sticking his stupid, rippled bald head into each cell, glancing around, and moving on.

I started to fidget, calculating how much time it would take for him to make his way down to the ground floor. Only a few seconds, not nearly enough to warn the Jenns without calling major attention to them. I panicked and thought about what would happen to them if they got caught . . . and then what they'd do to me if I was the reason they got caught.

Fuck, fuck, fuck, I whispered with every stair he bounded down. I'd never seen him display an ounce of athleticism, but here he was basically downhill skiing.

As Garza reached the last step, he grabbed the railing to spin his body around the corner right into the nearest cell—the one next to the clit that wouldn't quit. With my heart racing I coughed loudly, hoping to catch someone's attention and buy me some time, but it went completely unnoticed.

He began to walk toward Jenn's cell and I panicked.

"AEEIIIIIII," I squealed at a decibel that could only be described as ungodly.

Officer Garza whipped around as I fell to the floor and started to convulse. I tried to roll my eyes into the back of my head, but that took way too much effort and gave me an instant headache, so I shut them as I shook my legs in what I hoped was a convincing display of epilepsy.

Garza ran toward me, paging medical through his walkie-talkie.

"Lockdown, everyone! Now!"

I squinted toward Jenn's cell and watched as #3 slipped out, glancing at me with wide eyes and walking swiftly toward her own bunk.

I continued to twitch and wheeze, drooling a bit for good measure, until I was confident that everyone was safe. When I started to "come to," Garza was kneeling next to me, face a little paler than before.

"Ferrell, are you okay? Can you hear me?"

"Wh-what happened?" I stammered.

"You had a seizure, medical is on their way. Don't move."

When he got up to let the nurses in I scanned the faces peering at me from inside their locked cells until I found Jenn's. She was smiling broadly with all her teeth, silently clapping for my breathtaking performance.

The next morning at 5:30 the overhead fluorescent lights (that never fully turned off) hummed bright with an alarming intensity.

I willed myself out of bed, practically oozing onto the floor, and gathered myself to stand at attention near the door. This was how every morning began, though not always at the same time—it was dependent on the day's CO and how generous they were feeling. I closed my eyes and swayed sleepily back and forth until I felt a mop shoved into my hands. While my cellie sprayed everything down with an unlabeled cleaning agent, I swabbed the five-by-nine cube that had become our home. After a quick inspection by the guard, bleary-eyed himself, we were allowed to climb back into bed and drift off to the astringent smell of bleach.

That afternoon, the first time that we had been out since my "episode," I was outside in the yard and the sun was shining. Against every dermatologist's advice, I lifted my face up toward it and let the rays envelop me, melanoma be damned. One of the Jenns sidled up next to me and took a few packs of Ho Hos out of her pants, pushing them toward me. They were warm from the heat of her crotch, and I greedily accepted and stuffed them down near my own.

"Aw, thanks. These are my fave." I paused. "And . . . what about the phone card?" I asked, trying to sound nonchalant, lest she think I was ungrateful for the snacks and renege on our original deal. In my experience, most of the women in the jail looked out for one another, but promises were only as good as someone's word, and words are notoriously unreliable. Jenn pulled the flimsy card out of God knows where and handed it over with a genuine smile. I took it and slid it into my breast pocket, the only one our uniforms had, meant to hold our photo ID cards that we were required to have on our person at all times (except when we were sleeping—then they had to be placed against the window, in case a guard wasn't familiar with our mugs). Jenn still had a toothy grin plastered on her face and gave me the universal symbol for eating pussy with a wink and walked away. I laughed aloud and felt strangely and unexpectedly grateful for life's amusing moments.

.The other women and I did what we could to make doing time fun: impromptu talent shows (if uncoordinated dance routines and semi-convincing magic tricks count as talents), speaking for days on end with poorly executed cockney accents, and con-couture fashion shows using our uniforms and bath towels to play dress-up. Most everyone participated in these childish activities regardless of age or tenure, because when you're infantilized day in and day out, it's easier—and a lot more entertaining—to lean into it. Some of the guards allowed us to go about our antics, the occasional one even cheering us on, whereas others would literally put us in time-out. I often wondered how society can expect inmates to *grow up* when they're trapped in a shitty daycare that is committed to teaching their charges absolutely nothing. It was entirely up to us to better ourselves, and that could be really fucking exhausting. But through it all we had something that the guards, the state, and the system could never take away from us. We had each other.

13

TRAILER TRASH

Three more months and a whole sweltering season passed, marked only by the dwindling amounts of sunlight that would dapple the concrete floors throughout the day. Fall had arrived and one crisp night, I was wondering if anyone would decorate for the holidays. I had popped a Benadryl and was drifting off imagining toilet paper snow scenes when Officer Shoals came over the intercom.

"Ferrell, I've got a surprise for you!"

I sat up with eyes wide and waited for him to tell me where I was headed. It wasn't uncommon for the guards to move people around to different cells (sometimes for legitimate reasons and sometimes to fuck with us). Not one month prior, my former cellie, Madyson, had been released and I got stuck with a first-timer crackhead. The first-timer part was far more annoying than the crackhead part and I had sweet-talked Shoals into swapping her with a friend of mine.

I started to put my belongings—many more than when I first got there—into my tote box. Stacks of letters and photos, some magazines, and of course the contraband hidden around the cell (candy and extra books, mostly).

Who was going to be my new cellie? Would I be on the top or bottom floor? Oh my god, what if they move me to another pod?!

The intercom crackled. "Ferrell! Do you want to go home or not?"

I perked up, my heart beating even faster.

"Home? Like . . . out of here?" I asked quietly, needing confirmation.

"Let's go, they're almost here to get you," Shoals said sharply.

I paused for a beat, dumbfounded, when I was startled by my shrieking cellie.

"BITCH, YOU'RE GOING HOME!" she yelled as she clapped. "Better not forget about me!" The plea of millions of incarcerated people.

Even though I was leaving, I still had to be handcuffed to walk through the never-ending corridors, until I was placed in a holding cell. With puppy dog eyes I held my wrists out, and the officer shrugged and then removed the cuffs. Minutes or hours went by, and I paced (two to three steps each way—the cell was much smaller than my regular one) as I waited for the administrative officers to move through the steps that would secure my freedom.

It was a bittersweet moment. I was saying goodbye to what had been my home for so many months. A place I was intimately familiar with; the contained sights, smells, and sounds and mind-numbing schedule were comforting in their predictability. Within confinement I felt free in ways I hadn't before: it was such a relief to not have to keep up with my multiple identities and countless lies. It was a place where I had not only witnessed and experienced pure hope and devastation, but was allowed to express it for the first time. I would deeply miss the women, many of whom I had truly fallen in love with. How could I make it without their support and daily affirmations? How was I to live without my compatriots, my community, my friends? And at the risk of sounding like a pig-loving traitor, I'd maybe even miss some of the guards. It's hard to let some of that shit go.

A door clanged open and an officer handed me my civilian clothes (referred to as such like I had come back from war, which is apt, I suppose). I shed my penal skin and let my own clothes envelop me. I was pleased that they fit so well as I had no clue how much I weighed, and since full-length mirrors weren't a thing in jail, there was a lot of room for surprise.

After I tied my shoes (with real motherfucking laces), it all hit me at once. I started to shake like an epileptic chihuahua. My life of structured routine was the exact fucking opposite of what I was about to step into. I shivered as my heart threatened to burst out of my chest, not from the cold of the concrete cell, but because I knew that now I had to face another kind of punishment: starting anew in the outside world.

A voice I didn't recognize cut through the silence over the

intercom. "Alright, Ferrell, you're out of here. Proceed down the hall and through both sets of doors. There's a pay phone before you exit. Good luck."

The door clanged open once again, the universe inviting me back into its chaos. I took a deep breath and started to step out of the cell—except that I couldn't. I was frozen in place.

"Ferrell, no one in their right mind would stay in there. Let's go!"

I shook my head back and forth, trying to clear my mind and reassemble my thoughts like they do in the cartoons.

"Okay, here we go," I said as I chose freedom.

At the far end of the parking lot, I waited for Madyson, whom I had called excitedly from the pay phone, with a *"Guess whoooo."* She was one of the girls who actually stayed in contact as she promised to do when she left, and even came to visit me a couple of times. She was what true friends are made of: understanding, like-mindedness, and on probation and parole.

There was a honk in the distance as her car tore through the parking lot and zoomed up to me. I heard Madyson shout from the driver's side window, "Get in, loser, we're going home!"

We pulled up to where Madyson lived with her mother: a small, quaint building that was part of a larger planned community of similar-looking small, quaint buildings. She unlocked the door and flipped on the lights. No one was home. I threw myself on the couch as she handed me a Go-Gurt from the fridge. I looked at it through wet eyes, as if I had never sucked goo out of a tube before. I tore open the plastic with my teeth, and its laceration started to ooze dark pink. I slurped it up.

"Oh wow, this is *incredible*," I said, not a stitch of hyperbole in my voice. "Truly one of the finest meals you could have offered me. I'm in heaven."

You acclimate to the real world faster than you'd think, but you still forget how to operate in a society now and then. The first week after my release I ate dinner from my bed—I preferred it that way. And I tucked my sheets in every morning, a trait I wish I could say continued through to the present day. I tried to be an exemplary house guest, hoping that my actions would reflect the gratitude I had for Madyson and her mom, even though she wasn't around much. I worried it had to do with my presence, but Madyson reassured me that wasn't the case and I was more than welcome.

The first couple of days of my newfound freedom were spent calling my family to let them know that I was out, catching up on unread emails that numbered in the thousands, and of course reaching out to the media. I contacted Lizzie Foster from *Inside Edition*, and she responded that her team could be in Salt Lake in a couple of days, if I was up for it. *What do I have to lose?* I thought. And more importantly, *What can I gain?*

It's extremely rare (and in many cases illegal) for subjects of news profiles and documentaries to receive monetary compensation. While I was in jail, every now and then a journalist would reach out and "donate" a few bucks to my commissary fund, but that's as far as it went. Being on the outside didn't change the situation much, but Lizzie agreed to provide me with an outfit and some makeup, and of course "the opportunity to get your side of the story out there."

I asked Madyson and her mom if it was okay to film the bulk of the interview at the house and they happily agreed. This was an exciting moment for all of us—*filmmakers from Hollywood* were coming to the suburbs of Holladay, Utah—and we rehearsed lines for an invisible audience in the living room.

Bright and early on the day of the shoot, as the cameras were being set up where we had practiced our mock trial for the court of public opinion, one of the producers drove me to Walmart. This was not what I had in mind when they told me that we'd be going shopping, but I'd take what I could get. In the juniors' clothing section, I flipped through the racks and landed on a sleeveless black top that framed my tattoo in what I thought was a respectable manner—I wanted to be taken seriously—but in retrospect was giving *front of house at a cheap steakhouse*. I grabbed a mismatched foundation, an alarmingly cheap shadow and blush palette, and an eyebrow pencil from the cosmetics aisle. The quality may have been questionable, but it was so many steps above using colored pencils and Jolly Ranchers as makeup that I was elated. Plus, I didn't even have to pay for (or steal) it!

When we returned to the house the rest of the crew was set to roll. They gave me fifteen minutes to get camera-ready, and I had to weave around light boxes and step over extension cords to get to the bathroom. With my face and hair as good as they'd ever be, a sound guy snaked the wire of a lavalier microphone up my shirt as the producer rattled off directions (speak in a regular volume at a measured pace, don't look directly in the camera, etc.), and gestured toward one of two chairs facing another. The interviewer and I sat, our knees so close that they were almost touching, and she asked if I was ready. I nodded and someone said "Action!" (Like in the movies!) While I tried to give thoughtful answers to probing questions, I was also trying to keep my eyes open in the face of the bright lights. It felt more like an interrogation than any of the real ones I had been through.

The cross-examination was quick, and after a few minutes the interviewer thanked me for speaking with her, someone called "Cut!" and the lights were shut off. I stood and took my first deep breath of the day, hoping that I did myself—and the incarcerated women I loved—some kind of justice. While the crew started to disassemble the equipment, I moved to take the mic off my shirt when the producer interrupted. She asked if I would be open to filming B-roll, silent footage that would accompany the interview, and I eagerly agreed. As nerve-wracking as the day had been, I didn't want it to end. I may not have received the star treatment I had been expecting, but this was my first foray into TV and film, and I was fascinated. The producer then asked if I would be open to filming the B-roll at the jail. "Outside of it, of course," she added.

As the production's rented van pulled into the parking lot of the adult detention center, the producer mused that it must feel empowering for me to be back there, this time with a film crew in tow. It didn't. It felt like misery and hopelessness and was haunted by all the living lost souls caged only a few feet away, many of whom

I knew. We pulled over toward the far end of the parking lot, and they got the footage they wanted of me walking away from the jail.

The piece never aired on TV and the only proof I have of it existing at all is a screenshot from *Inside Edition*'s website. At the time I was crushed: I had envisioned the interview changing the path of my life toward a direction I wasn't able to forge on my own. I can see now that it was all for the best, because as much as I believed I knew about myself and the system, I really had no idea.

One afternoon, two and a half weeks into my new reformed life, my probation officer came to do a home visit and he brought bad news along with him: someone who is on probation cannot live with another person who is also on probation. Now, this law is skirted regularly and with relative ease in many cases, but it turns out that Madyson's mom had also been in trouble and was struggling with her own legal issues. I knew I needed to get out of there for all of our sakes.

After a bit of groveling, the state of Utah allowed me to go to Arizona for two weeks, where I would be allowed to stay at my mom's house (after more groveling) to figure out my next steps. I had no other options—my dad refused to take me back in, and I didn't have any other friends I could stay with who hadn't been in jail with me. After the fourteen days were up, under no exceptions, I had to return to Utah and find a place to live on my own.

Throughout my stint in jail, my mom continued to write letters and send cards for every holiday I missed. We talked on the phone sparingly (mostly because calls were so damn expensive), and

I couldn't wait to hear her voice in person. But when I landed in Phoenix my worst suspicions were confirmed: my relationship with my family was forever changed by the horrible all-encompassing shitshow I had put them through. And what did I expect? That they would welcome me back with open arms (they did) and promise to love me no matter what (they did)? Still, on the drive to their home, we danced nimbly around our words, my mom's voice breaking when she recounted a time that a reporter had tracked her down for a comment, and how she had seen some of my leaked nudes. Her disappointment weighed me down more than any shackles ever could, and I knew that it would be a long time before she trusted me again.

That afternoon, sitting in their xeriscaped backyard surrounded by cacti that could thrive in even the harshest of conditions, I felt like I was doing time in another way. The clock never stopped ticking, and I was counting down to another miserable unknown.

As the two weeks came and went, my mom and stepdad desperately tried to get me back on track. They had helped me so many times over the years, to varying degrees of success and appreciation, and the final result was still yet to be seen. I promised them I was going to be okay, that I had a plan. I told them that I was going to stay with friends in Salt Lake City who were job-possessing professionals who didn't do any drugs and were good, honest people. My mom didn't ask too many questions, and I don't know if she actually believed me. If she did, she shouldn't have.

I had found a couple with a small, dirt-cheap open room on

Craigslist, not too far from the probation and parole office I was legally required to check into once a week. In response to my email inquiry I had received a blurry scan of a photo of a woman (presumably the wife) in well-worn lingerie, her chapped nipples poking through the fabric of the lacy teddy I could only guess was the finest that Spencer's Gifts had to offer.

We swapped a couple more emails and they agreed to pick me up from the airport when I arrived. The photo wasn't mentioned, but I knew that they knew that I knew what was going on. I've found that in times of despair, the greatest gift you can give yourself is ignorance (it is bliss, after all). My best-case scenario was living with a couple of dusty old swingers.

At the Phoenix Sky Harbor Airport, I hugged my mom goodbye. "Bye, Mom, I love you so much. Thanks for everything," I said, meaning every damn word I said.

"I love you, honey," she said. "Make good choices."

Make good choices. A phrase my mom has said throughout my entire life—beginning as a Choose the Right–like "reminder" that God was always watching. If he was, I hope he liked melodramas.

The metal tube that carried me hurtled through the sky and then slowed down and was met by the frozen ground of the SLC airport. Déjà vu took hold and I waved my hands in front of my face, making sure that they weren't handcuffed like they had been the last time I made this pilgrimage.

I waited at arrivals until a massive, shiny black pickup truck, new and expensive, pulled up in front of me. The Wife confirmed who they were by saying my name three times in a row, while looking me up and down. They were longer in the tooth than I expected . . . or maybe they were actually in their thirties and drank gallons of Mountain Dew and smoked fifteen packs a day. Hard to say either way, but their skin looked like it had been sheared off a lizard that had died from dehydration and was left out to rot for ten days. The Husband got out and easily hoisted my luggage into the bed of the truck. I wondered if he had ever used sunscreen a day in his life. He opened my door and gave me a slightly too-long hug, rubbing his spiral ham–size hands over my lower back.

"I'm so glad you're here," he whispered into my hair.

We drove the forty-five minutes from the airport in relative silence. My thoughts raced and I couldn't focus on a single one without getting all wound up, so I did what I have always done to cope: I went inward. So deep into the abyss that is my soul, my brain and body became detached, not even in the same fucking atmosphere. My hands shook violently and I tried to calm myself by coming up with an exit plan in the event that they decided to drown me in the briny waters of the Great Salt Lake.

We pulled off the highway and drove into a dingy-looking trailer park.

"Welcome to our humble abode," The Wife said.

There have been *many* times in my life that I've asked myself, "How the fuck did I get here?" and this was now at the tippy-top of the list. I mustered all the composure I could and swung myself out of the truck, airborne for a flash before my feet hit the gravel driveway.

The Couple showed me around their modest trailer. Outside of a few mystery stains on the carpet, it was a lot tidier than I expected. I had imagined hoarders-level filth; cat bones hidden in piles of dirty diapers and rotting meat in the bathtub.

"Your room is back here . . . right next to ours," The Husband said.

The room reminded me of my closet in Brooklyn, small but consistent in its boxy design and lack of shelf space. I put my suitcase down on the bed and looked around. There were photos of random kids with big, toothy grins on the dresser, and hideous orange-and-brown blankets from the '70s on the bed, and there was fake wood paneling on the walls. The room looked exactly how it smelled (mothballs and stale cigarettes), a phenomenon I have yet to experience in such a way since.

"Well," The Wife said, "we're real glad to have you here." And then, "Don't fuck us over, because we may seem nice but we don't have to stay that way."

I was appreciative of the threat and glad for it to be out in the open. Communication is the key to making good choices.

That evening after watching a bit of local news (which is a great way to find out what kind of people your proxy captors are, and where they stand on low-fat cottage cheese, the right to own guns regardless of age, and college football), I asked if they might have a computer I could borrow. They did, and I could use it for thirty minutes.

I clicked on my inbox and saw that I had a "what's up?" email from a guy named Noah whom I had sent nudes to with his name scrawled across my belly, and one from Madyson. We missed each other but knew that we had told one another too many lies to continue a real-world relationship.

As I opened an email from someone who appeared to be a Nigerian prince, I felt a wide and warm hand slide into my shirt and down my chest. I jumped and looked up at The Husband, who pinched my nipple when I asked him what he was doing. I started to squirm, trying to get away from him, but his arm was so big I couldn't get it out of my shirt, which he most definitely used to his advantage. He held me down and pinched again, hard. I screamed at him to get the fuck away from me at a decibel that startled him into compliance.

"Easy, easy," he said as he slowly removed his hand, making sure to cop one last feel. He walked backward out of the room and shut the door behind him.

The next morning before anyone woke up, I left. I wasn't sure where to go, and after hours of dragging my suitcase from McDonald's to Burger King to Wendy's, I found myself at the gas station where The Wife worked. I was so fucking desperate that I had gone to my assaulter's wife for advice.

"Heard you're moving," she said as she watched me warily.

"Yep," I said rigidly as I scanned the sodas by the register.

"Well, it's a shame it didn't work out. You good?"

"Yep."

She looked at me with hard pity, but said nothing.

"Actually, I'm not good. I don't know where to go," I said pathetically.

"Then why would you leave a warm bed?"

I stayed silent and her eyes softened, her lips relaxing from their scowl.

"I know of a hotel not too far from here," she said. "Weird place, but they'll definitely have an open room. The guy who owns it is a little eccentric but will work with you."

"Can you print directions for me?"

"Don't be a spoiled bitch. You take a right out of here and then walk a few miles and it will be on the right side. The Kurt Hotel."

I rocked back on my heels and walked out of the gas station, muttering a thanks, knowing that I'd never see her weathered face or chapped nipples again.

After a long walk ("a few miles" was not an understatement), I arrived at my destination. I quickly realized that this wasn't any ordinary hotel—it was a work of art. Not one that you'd find in a museum, but a sight to behold. From the outside it wasn't anything special, but it was huge, easily taking up a whole block. Upon walking into the lobby the first thing that caught my attention was a massive fish tank running along the entirety of one of the long walls. I peered in but couldn't see any fish, only algae and bubbles from the oxygen being pumped in by a complicated-looking apparatus.

I spun around, looking at the comfortable furniture that was much nicer than I expected. There wasn't a front desk so I wandered into an adjacent room, which was like a clubhouse—large-screen TV, more comfortable furniture, and a huge kitchen. As I was taking it all in, a ball of fur whizzed past me, almost taking me out. Two more balls of fur followed, puppies frolicking with seemingly free range of the place. I tried to scoop one up for cuddles, but it turned into liquid in the way only puppies can and wriggled out of my hands.

"That's Emory. You'll never truly catch her," I heard a voice say. "Even when you have her, she's never really yours."

I laughed and turned toward a gentleman who, if I had to guess, was in his mid-sixties.

"Then Emory and I are cut from the same cloth," I said.

"I'm Gareth, the owner of this fine establishment. How can I help you?"

I took the check that I had been carrying around out of my back pocket. It was issued to me by the state, for the amount of my commissary balance and the cash I had walked into jail with, about $300.

"How many nights can I get for this?" I asked as I slid it over to him across the granite kitchen counter.

Gareth looked it over and then looked me over and invited me into his office.

"With a discount I can give you a week here in one of the economy rooms," he offered.

"Okay, great. Thank you so much." I paused, hoping my appreciation was palpable. "Um, by chance, is there any work that needs to be done around the hotel? I'm really proficient at a lot of things, and need a place for longer than a week. Maybe indefinitely . . . I don't know . . . I'm figuring stuff out as I go," I explained earnestly.

Gareth thumbed his chin and spun the check around. After a few seconds he cleared his throat and asked, "Can you cook?"

I nodded enthusiastically. Gareth smiled and took me to a room and handed me the key. The space was sparse and had a concrete floor (not in a cool Brooklyn way, in a *this is what you get* way) and the smallest bathroom known to man.

"It's not much," Gareth said, "but it's not the street."

"It's perfect," I—a person who had lived in a closet and a cell—responded.

"Make yourself comfortable, and when you're ready, come on out and I'll give you the grand tour and introduce you to some folks."

The door shut behind him and I took great pleasure in locking the door instead of having it locked for me. I threw myself on the bed, *very springy*, and smiled at my great fortune. Gareth had agreed to let me stay there if I cooked dinner for him and the long-term guests nightly. He didn't need to know that I could barely boil water.

The hotel was even larger than I thought, and not all of the rooms were as bleak as mine. As you climbed the winding staircase up to the second and third floors, the fixtures in the hallway became nicer, as did the addition of a soft (mostly clean) carpet.

"Want to see something cool?" Gareth asked with an almost manic edge.

"Do I have to say yes or no before you tell me what it is?"

He grabbed my hand and pulled me through a door into a suite that was unexpectedly chic. Fancy, up-to-date appliances and about five times the space my little concrete cave had. There was a sitting room, dining room, proper kitchen, and bedroom.

"Damn! I didn't realize the rooms up here were like *this*," I said, trying to hide the indignation I felt.

Am I not good enough to be in one of these?

"It's true that they're nicer than the lower level, but this one is especially well taken care of because it is mine."

A quick chill went down my spine after I realized that I had unwittingly come into his room and he was still holding my hand tightly.

I coughed and reeled my hand back toward my body with lightning speed, like a viper in reverse.

"You said you had something you wanted to show me?"

Don't be your old man penis, don't be your old man penis, don't be your old man penis.

"Come check this out," he said as he walked over to a small closet-turned-office and popped a panel off the wall.

I peered in, glancing around the darkness, trying to guess what I was looking at when, with a flicker and a quiet *whirrr*, several bright lights lit up as if on cue.

"Oh, holy shit," I breathed.

"We've got indicas, sativas, hybrids, and I'm experimenting with a form of wax," Gareth explained. "This is obviously top-secret and I trust very few people to come into my personal life like this."

He paused.

"Um, well, I'm honored." I blushed. "This is nuts."

It was, at the time, the most amount of marijuana I had seen in one place (plant, flower, or otherwise).

I went to stroke a leaf and Gareth pulled me back and replaced the panel.

"I said that I trust you, but it goes both ways and won't last forever," he said as he guided me out of the room.

As I tried to process what he might have meant, the door closed quietly in my face and I headed down the stairs to figure out what to make for dinner. It felt good to be trusted again, but what good is trust if it's mired in doubt?

"Okay, gentlemen, tonight we have pesto cavatappi, a Caesar salad, and garlic bread. And don't worry, I'm making a second batch of everything, so eat up!"

The fifteen or so men standing around the kitchen clapped politely before bum-rushing their way toward the food, sending the loose tendrils of steam in all directions.

I had been at the Kurt Hotel for two weeks, and I was getting the hang of the whole cooking for an army thing. And that wasn't a turn of phrase—the majority of the long-term guests were former military on contract as civilians at the nearby Dugway Proving Ground. They were brash oafs who drank their moral woes away on the daily, but they were respectful enough, and certainly enjoyed the company of a woman (even if it was only to complain about the one they had at home). And I'd be lying if I said I didn't enjoy their company and attention. Cooking for this ragtag group of mercenaries had given me a sense of purpose. I had groceries to collect, a schedule to adhere to, hungry people who were counting on me for nourishment of body, mind, and soul. Okay, that might be taking it a little too far, but I *know* they were listening to what I was saying when they weren't asking me to flash them.

Gareth and I got along fine and he certainly held up his end of the bargain, but unlike the cavalry, he wasn't so forthright in his intentions, which gave me the creeps. I chose to ignore the salacious leers and other red flags, telling myself that I had been locked up too long and my predator radar was wonky. Plus, he loaned me a laptop and let me take his car to Park City to attend the Sundance Film Festival. So what if I caught him rubbing his wrinkly hand over his crotch every now and then? This was the best option I had.

As I was cleaning up the night's meal, listening to inane sports chatter in the background, I thought I saw something move out of the corner of my eye. I spun around, but couldn't find anything and told myself that I was tired and imagining things. The evening before, the guys had kept me up with five rounds of Never

Have I Ever. Usually I slay, but jail life and military life aren't that different, so it went on deep into the night. Eventually I came out victorious, wiping the remaining four people out with "never have I ever killed a person."

I finished putting the dishes away and polished the counter clean. As I was turning off the lights I again thought I saw something moving. I shuffled back to my room and went to unlock the door, but it swung open as soon as I touched the handle. I could have sworn I locked it . . . but I was also juggling a cookbook, laptop, and a jar of manuka honey I had swiped from Whole Foods when I left, so who knows.

Nothing in the room looked like it had been touched; everything was where I had left it. I shrugged it off and brushed my teeth and washed my face (a feat in that small-ass sink). As I was patting my cheeks, a dry chill ran up my spine.

Yes, I had *definitely* locked the door, because my hands were so full that I had almost dropped the keys. As I climbed into bed, I couldn't help but feel like I was being stalked.

14

MURDER-SUICIDE

I jolted from bed in a moment of panic, stubbing my toe on the goddamn floor in the process. Confused and in pain, I wildly rotated my head trying to piece together my surroundings. *Where am I?*

The dresser didn't look familiar, the TV mounted on the wall was bigger than the one I remembered, and underneath my sore pinky toe I felt carpet. *Okay, but really, where am I?*

A loud snore startled me and I looked back at the bed, where a bearded man was so deeply asleep that if I hadn't just heard him fart out of his nose I would have thought he was dead. And maybe that I had killed him in my fugue state.

Elliot, I remembered. His name was Elliot.

I realized that I was in his bedroom, located in the basement of a large house in a nice suburban neighborhood outside of Salt Lake City called Eagle Mountain, at the foot of the Wasatch range. I had been here, in this house, many times in the past month. The bedroom was sparse, void of any sentimentality whatsoever. In fact, the entire house had no pictures, mementos, or other personal effects; in their places were many nearly-always-drunk government contractors, Elliot being one of them.

I made a huge mistake, I thought in the voice of Gob Bluth from *Arrested Development* as I rushed to put my clothes back on. Sprinting out of the room, I climbed the stairs and knocked gently on a door.

"Hey, Ant, can I come in?" I asked while opening the door, not waiting for a reply.

"What's up?" Ant asked.

"I gotta get back to the hotel. Can you drive me? We can stop at Maverick and I'll buy you an egg sammy."

"Fine," he said, "but only for the egg sammy."

Paul Antony was a former sergeant in the US Army who suffered a traumatic brain injury (and a subsequent bout of severe depression) that took him out in the form of an honorable discharge. When he got back to the States from Iraq, he didn't know what else to do besides what he had been doing since he was eighteen years old. So he found himself shaking hands with the devil and working as a drone pilot for a private defense company.

I had met Ant at the Kurt Hotel, when he was walking through the lobby holding a print by David Shrigley. I lasered in and jogged to catch up to him, desperate for connection with anyone who had even a kernel of individuality.

"Shrigley, right?" I asked, nodding toward the print.

"Yeah!" he said excitedly. "Love his shit."

We walked toward the kitchen together.

"So, what are you doing here? Are you, like, the cook?" Ant asked.

"Yeah, something like that. Many hats, etcetera, etcetera," I laughed.

"Well then, do you want to make me something? Oh, God— that sounded horrible, I'm joking. I'm a feminist!"

That day we ended up talking for five hours, giggling as we watched the hotel pups run around, taking an intermission to pee and grab more snacks. Ant was from the Bible Belt and had hopes of becoming a writer; his father was an abusive alcoholic and his mother was all of that but worse. He had channeled the entirety of his rage toward his parents, school, and church. All he wanted was to blow up his world, same as me. He just took it a tad more literally.

Ant's story was a familiar one—many men and women had fallen into the same trap over the decades. As part of an arrangement with the defense company he worked for, the US government— aka the taxpayers, aka you and me—put the boys up for the duration of their stay at the base. They had the choice of either a decent hotel (unlike my concrete room at the Kurt, Ant's room was on the second floor and had carpet) or a shared house with roommates.

And like a man's choice in shoes, you know if you want to date, marry, or fuck the guy who picks the hotel room over the house—which is why my world spun that morning. Elliot was not my preferred room. He felt nothing like home.

The first time I met Elliot his eyes were rolling in the back of his head, drunk as a baby elephant in a distillery, and he refused to shake my hand, staring at it uselessly when I extended it toward him. It was obvious after a couple of nights that this was part of his routine. These guys were used to order, and their inexperience with free will showed. They were backed by a lot of money, a lot of time, and a need for escapism. So, naturally, they got fucked up every night.

I was hanging out at the house a lot because not only were these dudes paying a lot of attention to me, but giving myself over to other people felt safe. Plus, they were good guys, for the most part. Or at least they meant well, and in some worlds that's as good as doing.

One night, once the house had settled, I went to the kitchen to grab a snack and a Coke and caught Elliot's glowing face illuminated by the bright light of the water dispenser, singing a song softly to himself. I tried to listen to what it was, but he stopped abruptly as soon as he saw me.

"Hi," I said. "Midnight munchies."

"Yeah," he replied softly, "I—"

"What were you singing? Anything I'd know?"

"Uh, you like . . . music?" he asked.

I stared at him dumbfoundedly and then rolled my eyes.

"Nope, don't like it. Never got it."

His turn to stare. We both smiled at the same time.

"I was singing this song by a band called Neutral Milk Hotel. Know 'em?"

To say I was shocked was an understatement. The guy who thought nice denim came from The Gap and wore sunglasses that made him look like a dollar-store Republican knew who lo-fi indie rock darlings Neutral Milk Hotel were? As I shoved pretzels into my mouth, choking them down a dry throat (never got my Coke), I smiled to myself and thought that maybe he wasn't so bad after all.

Fast-forward to running out of his bedroom like a banshee whose pubes were on fire. There were probably a million reasons I was freaking out, but top of mind was that I had started to catch feelings. There was something dark and mysterious about Elliot, and I had an undeniable attraction to the rubble that was his bombed-out heart. Plus, we were both wards of the state—a reminder that jail and the military aren't all that different. So, of course, I did the only thing I was good at: I set out to sabotage myself.

After Ant dropped me off at the hotel, I realized that I only had twenty minutes to get to the probation and parole office for my weekly check-in. I popped up to Gareth's office, hoping he'd let me take his Oldsmobile Cutlass for a spin, but when I got close I heard fraught whisper-shouting. I looked around before putting my ear to the door. I wasn't usually such a snoop, but after the incident with my room being unlocked I had started to notice weird things around the hotel. Padlocked cabinets, calls from blocked numbers that Gareth documented with an old-school tape recorder, and a bank deposit bag that never made it to the bank.

I was about to leave when the door swung open and a skinny woman with pockmarks all over her face almost barreled into me.

"What the fuck are you looking at?" she spat as she hurtled by. Gareth appeared behind her.

"Kari, what are you doing here?" he asked sternly.

"I . . . I have to make an appointment and I'm running late. I was wondering if I could take your car for an hour. I'll fill it up with some gas."

Gareth sighed and shrugged, his eyes red. "Sure. Let me get the keys."

He closed the door and left me waiting in the hall, which I thought was odd, but Gareth had always been a private person. What was he hiding? Was he actually hiding *any*thing? Being a shifty miscreant made me assume that everyone else was a spinner of yarns, too. If you lie to yourself enough, you become the only truth and no one else is to be trusted.

The door popped open again and Gareth tossed the keys at me.

"I have to leave here at 5:00 P.M., don't be late," he said. "Don't forget the gas."

I ran out of the hotel and sped my way to my babysitter's office.

"Sandy, I'm here!" I screamed as I walked in. "With thirty seconds to spare!"

The receptionist contorted her features into what I think was supposed to be a scowl, but her pleasantly plump face and kind eyes betrayed her.

"You're lucky, missy, Officer Scanlon was about to head out. TYLER! Kari's here by the skin of her teeth!"

Ty Scanlon was in his mid-forties and used to be a beat cop back when that was still a thing. In recent years, community policing had morphed into a different beast, and so he was relegated to a desk job as a probation officer. He liked to reminisce about the good ol' days of manhandling perps and busting gang operations, but I think he preferred sitting in an air-conditioned office, shooting the shit with Sandy, and watching syndicated fake court case reality TV shows.

"Ferrell, I didn't think you were going to make it." He smiled.

Much like most other adults in my life, I had wooed Officer Scanlon and Sandy into liking me, trusting me. But should they like me? Should they trust me? I was always questioning my own intentions, thinking I was scamming even when I wasn't. Another side effect of being a shifty miscreant.

I walked into the back office and plopped down into my usual chair and answered all of the usual questions. *Have you been arrested since the last time we saw one another? Are you still at the same address? Are you gainfully employed? Have there been any new charges brought against you? Do you have an extra minute to chat?*

The last question caught me off guard and alarm bells started ringing in my skull.

"Sure, uh, what is it?" I asked nervously.

"We've received complaints that the owner of the Kurt Hotel is acting erratically. There are allegations that he's harassing tenants. Have you seen or heard anything that corroborates this?"

"I mean, not really," I said. My palms started to sweat. "Gareth is a *total* fucking weirdo, that's for sure, but seems pretty harmless."

"Have you ever had an inkling that illegal activity was taking place on the property?"

I thought of the marijuana plants growing in the walls, behind the hidden panel.

"No, not that I can think of."

"Do you have any reason to believe that you are being spied on or watched while on the premises?" Officer Scanlon asked.

"What the fuck?" I asked. "Why? Is that a thing that's happening?"

"A grievance was filed with the city a few weeks ago, before you arrived. All claims are alleged and nothing has been proven one way or another . . . but that's why I'm asking around. To try to get to the bottom of this."

I thought of the door that I swore I had locked and goose bumps infested my arms.

"I haven't seen anything, but I'll keep an eye out," I replied, not wanting to betray Gareth on an alleged whim.

Officer Scanlon thanked me and walked me to the exit. When I got back into the Oldsmobile, I sat on my hands to stop them from shaking. I opened the glove compartment and middle console, finding nothing but crumpled-up receipts and a brown gummy substance that was maybe a liquid in a past life.

I stared at my phone in my lap, flipping it over and over and over, trying to figure out how scared I actually felt. My feelings couldn't be trusted. I needed a second opinion. I dialed a number and it rang and rang, my mom's voice eventually cutting through the noise, prompting me to leave a message. I hung up and dialed another number.

"Hello?"

"Hey, Elliot, it's Kari. I gotta run something by you . . ."

After I returned to the Kurt I tossed Gareth the keys as he got in the car to head wherever he was going. As he drove away, I wondered if he had been watching me in that cold, dark hotel room this entire time. Had he witnessed a couple of nights before, when I had to stop masturbating because I couldn't stop crying uncontrollably? Had he seen me lying on the floor, staring at the ceiling, wondering if I could be fixed?

At 2:00 the next morning, I stood outside in the parking lot with my suitcase, waiting for my knight in shining armor(ed SUV) to come and save me. Elliot pulled up and gave me a quick hug, threw my stuff in the trunk, and hopped back into the driver's seat.

He looked deep into my eyes and asked, "Ready to go home?"

15

HAN BALL

Life moved fast after I moved away from Gareth and the accusations against him. I started writing professionally—in the sense that I was getting paid for it, sporadically and usually in pennies—on a more full-time basis, making the dreams I had years ago in New York City a reality. The fact that I was often writing about butt sex and my thoughts on real dolls was neither here nor there, the simple act of doing was fulfilling and gave me a sense of purpose. I may not have been putting pen to paper for *The New Yorker* or *The Atlantic* or even *The Huffington Post*, but it didn't matter, I was a goddamn *writer*.

In the beginning of my budding relationship with Elliot, I had thought our connection was fleeting. We'd share a fun few weeks together before he journeyed to the Middle East to do things that he couldn't talk about (not that I would have wanted to know anyway), and then I thought I'd never see him again. But things took a serious turn after he left for Afghanistan: we were long distance and we talked as much as possible. And we were very much in love—his crazy complimented my crazy and vice versa; we understood one another with the kind of strange trust that can only be given in times of true despair, and in our case that was the relationship itself.

Since I had been such an exemplary parolee, I was able to transfer my probation from Salt Lake City to New York City. I felt like the first time around I hadn't actually lived there, because the life I'd led was a lie. This was an opportunity to establish myself as the new me, the Kari who was carried on grounded legs, rooted in truth and new beginnings.

I knew that this was it, this was my last chance and I couldn't fuck it up . . . and I really, truly believed that I wouldn't. I was finally forming real relationships with real people, I felt supported and loved, and I had a dude—whom I didn't even have to lie to, nor did I want to—who wanted to support and take care of me. In fact, ironically, it was my honesty that had won him over.

In the hours before I was to board the flight that would take me back to the Big Apple, I was sitting at a desk in a dingy little classroom in a strip mall, situated between an orthodontist and a pest control business, taking a government-mandated course on the pitfalls of theft. I stared at the crude letters that had been scratched into the wood and was reminded of the holding cell at the courthouse. It represented a place and life that already felt so unfamiliar that I struggled to recall what the cool metal of the handcuffs felt like against the bones of my wrists.

"Now, what are some things you can do when you get an urge to commit a crime?" the mustachioed man at the front of the room asked lazily.

I rolled my eyes as the instructor asked, "Anyone?" What a joke this whole broken system was. These classes benefited no one but the government, which got to collect a couple hundred bucks from each unwilling participant. Fortunately for me, it was the very last thing I had to take care of. All that separated me from my new-new-new life was this class and a whiteboard stained with lists of Unhealthy Thinking Habits.

After the class was over, I halfheartedly thanked the instructor and grabbed my suitcase. I took one look back toward the shopping center and stared at the sign for the pest control company that featured a traitorous cartoon rodent holding a spray gun, ready to murder his own kind. The old me would have related to that self-sabotaging whiskered creature, but the new me was no rat. *Good riddance*, I thought, as I walked toward the car that would whisk me away toward my destiny.

It didn't take me long to move my stuff into the East Village apartment I'd share with a sympathetic former roommate. He was a half-deaf record-collecting hoarder whose small space was full to the brim with incredible first pressings of albums from musicians I had never heard of, but knew were important. I was so fortunate to have people like him in my life, those who knew who I was, but saw me for whom I had become. They believed in the good in me, and I began to realize that it was because I *did* have good in me. I clung to that truth, and the near-constant internal struggle with impulsivity that I had become so familiar with dissipated.

Through a touch of embellishment to my résumé (as opposed to the considerable embellishment of résumés past), I eventually found a job as an executive assistant at one of the world's largest consulting firms. It felt good to be (mostly) honest in my interviews, unlike the one at *VICE* where I rattled off lie after lie. The work was boring, but I excelled at it. I was a people pleaser, I lived to serve, my colleagues loved me, and for the most part I was happy. There was nothing that I wanted more than to fade into obscurity and live a normal life.

But normalcy wasn't in my DNA. The facade may have been there, but the foundation was always entrenched in batshit-off-the-wall insanity. Nothing about me or my life was normal. Even the run-of-the-mill events in my life were tinged with chaos.

Elliot and I decided to get married when I was twenty-three and he was twenty-five. We were only babies, but with every new day we were growing up, together. We absolutely loved one another, and Elliot also wanted to make sure that I would be taken care of if anything happened to him while he was overseas. He came home for thirty days out of every six months, and one cool summer night, he proposed to me in front of the retro *Die Hard* game at our favorite arcade, and we moved our relationship toward *next of kin* with protagonist John McClane's blessing.

Elliot went back to Afghanistan and we struggled to grasp the reality of a relationship where one person was gallivanting around, dancing on tables with bottle service and free drugs, and the other person was sleeping in a tent while air raid sirens sounded into the night. It wasn't fair, but it was a sacrifice that he made because he loved me. As I waited months for him to set foot back on US soil, I planned our wedding and sent out e-vites that implored our loved ones to "Be There When We Drop This Shit."

Our nuptials were simple—by that time I had moved us into our own apartment in Williamsburg, and we threw a small ceremony on our roof, the New York City skyline sparkling in the distance. We were married by one of our best friends who got ordained for the occasion and subsequently launched Zach Mack's Wedding Shack. We didn't write our own vows and Zach read the words "til death do us part" off a second-gen iPad.

Later that night, for the first time as Mr. and Mrs. Ensor (though it went against all of my feminist sensibilities, I had taken Elliot's surname in hopes of separating myself from my maiden name), we held what we really cared about: a rager at a place on Metropolitan Avenue that was a motorcycle garage by day and bar by night. Again, the *hipster* part of the moniker I was trying to shed wasn't totally unfounded. All of our dear friends, many of whom I had met and worked with at Gawker and *VICE*, attended.

The party went late into the night and was the impetus for a three-some (not us!), an arrest (not me!), and more drunken mistakes than we could count.

A couple of weeks after our party the venue closed. We found out that they were never licensed as a bar and were operating il-legally. They had lied to us, and that seemed like the most auspicious and appropriate start to our marriage. It was perfect.

Elliot was meant to go back overseas for one more stint, but he quit his job because he didn't morally agree with what he was doing. The journey of overcoming *his* past was ignited by the flames that engulfed the top-secret files he burned in the yard. Plus, he had a wife at home now.

It was my turn to take care of Elliot while he figured out what he wanted to do with his life (which included enrolling in the photography program at Parsons and a stint as an art handler). I continued to work good job after good job, until I was fired when someone ultimately figured out who I was—or at least who they thought I *still* was—but I always found another, better position.

We adopted a pit bull with baggage, Radley, who gave us a kind of purpose that only comes with taking care of another living creature, and we continued to foster our relationship with each other, our families, and our friends. We went on lovely vacations, we lived in a nice apartment, and by all accounts we thrived. But my inner turmoil still had its poisonous claws sunk deep into my body. I struggled to truly accept my past, who I had been, who I was. After putting it off for years, I finally pulled the theoretical trigger (to stop me from pulling the literal trigger?) and made an appointment to see a therapist.

What took you so long? you may ask, and if you ever discover the answer, please tell me. And if you could, present it in the form of a song and dance number, because maybe then I'll pay attention.

As I entered the nondescript building on 14th Street and Fifth Avenue for my first session, my stomach turned flips and I could hear my heartbeat bouncing between my ears. The ride in the elevator up to the eleventh floor was truly glacial, and I started to question my choice (which was a frequent feeling that I probably needed to tackle in therapy). The door slid open with a *ding*, and I paused before stepping out. *I mean, I'm already here . . . may as well . . .*

"Kari, nice to meet you. I'm Will," the kind white man in his mid-fifties at the door said as he extended his hand toward me.

"Hi, I'm Kari," I said, as if we hadn't already established this through our emails.

"Alright, have a seat, let's get started. Tell me about yourself. Why are you here? What made you seek therapy?"

I glanced around the small office, my eyes stopping at the short bookcase filled with all the texts you'd expect (the DSM-5, *The Power of Habit, Zen and the Art of Motorcycle Maintenance*), a box of Kleenex, and a Dunder Mifflin paperweight. There was an Eames chair for him (how very typical) and the choice of a small gray sofa or cushionless wooden chair for me.

I chose the sofa and took a deep breath. "Well, I'm adopted from Korea, but honestly that hasn't really affected me at all."

Will didn't respond, so I kept going.

"I wanted to get that out of the way. So you know that we don't need to focus on all of that."

"And what is it that you *do* want to focus on?" Will asked patiently.

"Well, I'm really anxious and work is a lot. You know, typical shit."

Over the next forty-five minutes, "typical shit" took on new meaning. I told him my story: the media, the jail time, the trailer park, and of course the lies. He listened intently, revealing little through his near-expressionless face. I couldn't read him so I kept talking. He seemed to be trying the same tactic used in interrogations, and what was all of this if not a full investigation?

Will barely said a word the entire session, and at the end I felt totally exhausted . . . and also . . . lighter? On my way out of his office I thanked him and quipped, "I'm about to become your most interesting patient."

As I left Will's office and stepped onto the bustling street, I let out a maniacal laugh. A mother pulled her small child away from me, which made me laugh even harder. I couldn't believe that I had put therapy off for so long. I hadn't expected to reveal all my cards to Will within the first session, but once I got started, I couldn't stop. *Damn*, I thought, *I am going to ace this whole therapy thing. I'm going to make it my bitch.*

As the weeks and sessions went on, we dove deeper. I came to terms with what I had known all along: that being adopted had left a huge hole in my past and subsequently my heart. Will encouraged me to join a support group for transnational adoptees. I scoffed. *Why would I need to do that? After all, I'm in therapy!* But, of course, the isolation continued to nag at me, especially knowing how easy it would be to join a meeting. I couldn't get myself to do it.

I compromised that I would sign up for the Korean adoptee group's newsletter, and I'd try to not immediately delete the emails as they fluttered into my inbox. Obviously my resolve and resistance dissipated and I dutifully ignored the communications, until one day I accidentally opened one of their emails with a verbal "Whoops!" I went to close it, but a line stopped me in my tracks.

"Han is a sense of helplessness because of the overwhelming odds against one, a feeling of unresolved resentment against injustices suffered, a feeling of acute pain in one's guts and bowels, making the whole body writhe and squirm, and an obstinate urge to take revenge and to right the wrong—all these combined."

The concept didn't make any sense to me, and yet I felt it made more sense than anything I had ever read before. It encapsulated everything I had held within my soft body for the past decade. It contained the tentacled monster that overshadowed my existence; each leg was a different malady, and they were all lashing out— trying to smack, suffocate, wallop whatever they could.

I highlighted "han," right-clicked, and commanded the Google machine to look it up, in hopes of finding deeper meaning and origin. *Where was the right-click for* my *life?* I wondered.

I stared at the first results and clicked on the link for the Wikipedia page. I read all of it, paused, read it all again, and then sobbed. The tears washed over me like a baptismal font, but this time I wasn't pledging myself to some imaginary God or doing it for the dead. I was being born anew through an ancient concept, one built upon suffering and misery.

The idea of being driven and defined by sadness was comforting and terrifying. *So*, I asked myself, *is this how it's going to be forever?* Despite my life improving dramatically after getting out of jail, the rigors of acclimating to the real world and a normal life had taken their toll, even after so many years. Why did I feel such discontent? I had everything, I had built myself a wonderful life, but I was so fucking selfish, I wanted more. I was ungrateful, I was spoiled. I was all of the feelings I had ever been made to feel.

There are a number of reasons why han is so prevalent in Korea, when the majority of other countries don't have a word to even remotely describe the feeling. The country was colonized by Japan for thirty-five years and afterward divided into two countries, the North and South, after the Korean War. These experiences have burrowed into the psyches of everyday citizens like a horny weevil and have become an essential element of Korean identity. As you could expect, han can be a powerful emotion that can motivate a person to take action, but it can also be debilitating if it's not expressed.

My own han had come through the loss of people I thought I loved but would never actually meet. I realized that not knowing is worse than not being, so I started to dive into my culture as much as I'd permit myself. But as interested as I was, I also didn't believe that I was *allowed* to feel annoyed or jilted or wronged, because I had inflicted that same thing upon so many others. Han is complicated and tricky, there to comfort you on occasion and crucify you the next.

I frequently mourned the relationships I lost, which felt so goddamn selfish. I questioned whether I felt that way because of how I had hurt the other person, or because I had hurt myself. It took some time, but in due course I realized that it was a little bit of both, and that was okay. We are not good or bad—we're a mix of all the feelings and we choose which one is allowed to poke its head above water. If it's ugly and monstrous, we do our best to push it back down and drown it out with love, understanding, and kindness. It's often easier said than done—it's not easy to examine yourself so deeply, and you often feel like the more you learn the less you actually know. But what is existence if not a continuous education? The beauty of a life record is that over time it, too, can be redacted and expunged.

16

RETURN TO THE MOTHERLAND

Over the next several months I dutifully marched into therapy every week. After some sessions I could swear that I was fixed and after others that nothing had changed at all. My world spun at one hundred miles per hour like a whirling dervish who snorted a line of Adderall, and at other times like its rotation was stuck in quicksand.

Elliot had decided photography wasn't his life's passion, so he dropped out of The New School and started working part-time at a friend's company doing search engine optimization. It paid virtually nothing but he enjoyed his work, and that made me happy. I was working as an executive/marketing assistant at a company developing an Alzheimer's drug, and though it wasn't the most enthralling work, it paid decently. Which is a good thing, because in my mind's eye, I was the breadwinner, the cash cow, the golden fuckin' goose.

So, when a random meeting showed up on my calendar with HR on a Friday afternoon, I knew what was about to happen. I knew that at thirty years old I was going to find myself fired from yet another job, because this wasn't my first time at the rodeo. I had been bucked off the horse time and time again, working random jobs at a variety of companies, falling on my ass from the trading floor of a global financial institution, the well-stocked cafeteria of a social media giant, and the makeup aisle of perhaps the largest beauty MLM in existence. Despite this, I kept getting back up, luring the horse in with ketamine-soaked apples, and jumping back into the saddle. The meeting was in two hours, so up until then I kept working, palms so sweaty that they left little puddles on the keyboard as I responded to emails sent from people who would never hear from me again.

The last several years of my life had been spent in paranoia—I felt like I was always waiting for the other shoe to drop, for someone to discover my true identity. My jobs were legitimate; I paid taxes, I had a 401(k), I went to happy hours at shitty midtown bars when I'd rather be doing literally anything else, but I never disclosed anything about my past. My record had been expunged due to a very favorable plea bargain, so background checks didn't set off too many alarms, but I always worried about people googling me. So, to be safe, I started going by my middle name professionally. It's a pretty common thing to do; the people responsible for hiring didn't think much of it, and most importantly, if a colleague searched for *Michelle Ensor*, the only people who would come up were a pharmacist from Daytona Beach and a teacher who may or may not be dead.

But I didn't stop there. I made sure to block all of my coworkers on social media. Any time there was a new hire, unbeknownst to them, part of their onboarding was me searching for them online and making sure we didn't have any mutual connections. I hid the gigantic tattoo on my chest, which was surprisingly easy, and I silently thanked whoever it was who first designed Claudine collars (presumably someone named Claudine). I was always hyperaware of my surroundings. When out at said happy hours, I would scan the room and make sure I positioned myself with my back toward the crowd, in case a former associate happened to be at the same bar.

All of this went through my head almost every minute of every day. Whenever my boss called me, my heart dropped, and I would think, *this is it*. But most of the time it wasn't it, she was simply asking for the results of a double-blind study or wondering where her lunch was. It all felt very reminiscent of when I was incarcerated and waiting to see the judge. Not knowing if the next day I'd still be in jail was kind of like not knowing if I'd have a job. But hadn't I paid the price? Hadn't I done my time? How was it fair that something that defined a person a decade ago could follow them around like Peter Pan's fucked-up shadow? It was a hard life to live, with the lies you told years ago begetting more lies in the present day.

Physically, I was tightly wound. My body was always contorted, hands in fists, shoulders up to the sky, legs shaking. I cruised along like this for a while. I dealt with it, talked to my therapist about almost nothing else, and lived a very charmed life of misery. Aside from the whole stress-of-needing-to-provide-for-my-family thing, I was thriving. I had, at that point, had many of my close friends for years, people noticed me less (or if they did, they stopped coming up to me), and I felt very fulfilled in most areas. I eventually came to terms with the fact that my "normal" might not look like anyone else's.

But as always, I was full of dualities, a form of code-switching that was in many ways my own undoing. I was running under the radar at work, but then putting it all on display on Instagram (and I mean *all*—what can I say, I love being thotty). I wanted to blend in but was also desperate to be acknowledged for being my own person. I was hiding in plain sight.

And though living like this was exhausting, I was good at it. Every year up until that point could be considered practice. So, even though my internal dialogue was frazzled, it all came naturally. Authenticity, surprisingly, has always been very important to me—I guess that at one point my authentic self just really fucking sucked.

Finally, it was time to meet my fate. I started packing up my things, slowly peeling the tape off a polaroid of Elliot and me, throwing the martini-shaped tape dispenser that a coworker had gifted me for Christmas, because—ha—they thought they knew me, into my bag. I took a deep breath, pushed my chair back, and stood up.

I walked past a row of windowed offices lining one wall, head held high. There was no point in being a sad sack at this moment. An executive looked up from his computer and his eyes followed me. I pretended not to notice. The door to the conference room was closed and its glass walls were concealed by blinds that I had never once seen drawn before.

I opened the door with shaking hands and saw Adam, a young guy around my age who was a member of general counsel. Next to him was Patrick from HR, the first person I interviewed with. We had connected over our love of live music and basketball. Patrick gestured toward the single empty chair positioned across from the two of them. As I sat, Adam opened a folder, pulled out a single piece of paper, and slid it face down along the table toward me.

I turned it over, and staring back was my all-too-familiar mug shot; my chest tattoo on full display, my full name *KARI MICHELLE FERRELL* spelled out with *Hipster Grifter* listed under "known aliases." And, of course, the words *MOST WANTED* at the top.

"It has come to our attention," Patrick said in a voice two octaves higher than normal. He cleared his throat and started over. "It has come to our attention . . . that there may have been some jail time."

The one-sided conversation that ensued was everything I had heard before. They couldn't keep me on board, my employment jeopardized existing relationships with clients and had a negative effect on internal morale, etcetera. I acknowledged that all of this was, unfortunately, true.

"Michelle, I really wish we didn't have to do this," Patrick said softly. And then, "I really liked you, and you were phenomenal at the job."

That night when I got home, Elliot was wiping down the counter with vigor. Mess stressed him out, which is laughable considering whom he married. I threw the blazer I had ripped off my body as soon as I was escorted out of the office by security (so unnecessary!) and my bag on the floor, then flung myself onto the couch.

"You know you can put your shit away," Elliot remarked.

"Oh, *can I?*" I snarled.

I scrolled on my phone and felt his eyes boring into my skull.

"Ugh, fine," I mumbled as I picked my things up.

"Thank you. Not so hard, was it? Anyway, how was work?"

"You know. Uneventful," I said, not ready to fess up to what happened, not ready to be that vulnerable.

Elliot nodded and continued to clean the kitchen.

Sunday night came around and I still hadn't told anyone that I was unemployed. Elliot and I were folding laundry (see, I helped sometimes!) and he reminded me that I had leftovers to take for lunch the next day.

"Yeah, about that . . ." I said.

We stopped folding.

"Yeah?" Elliot asked.

"Yeah," I replied.

"Fuck."

He pulled me in for a hug while I cried into his shoulder. I didn't deserve him. I didn't deserve this life. I deserved to struggle. This was karmic retribution.

I must have been saying all of this in between my blubbering, because Elliot kept repeating, "That's not true," over and over while stroking my hair. I stopped and looked at him helplessly.

He returned my gaze and said with a smile, "I guess we should have bought the cheap toilet paper."

On Monday I hit the ground running and by Wednesday, I'd set up three interviews for the following week. I needed a job for all the reasons people need one, but there may have been a little part of me that was worried that I'd resort to my old ways, so I wasn't letting that become even an iota of an option.

After a few weeks of multiple interview rounds I was offered two jobs: one as a digital marketing manager at a boutique agency that specialized in the insurance space and a marketing specialist at a social media company whose bread and butter was disappearing images. If only parts of my life could vanish after twenty-four hours, too.

The one at the social media company was by far the more appealing of the two, but I knew that if I took it I'd spend more time worrying about being caught. It disturbed me that that's how I thought of it—*being caught*, as if I were trying to do anything but have a regular, normal-ass career. The insurance job was a boring, archaic, MPS (male, pale, and stale)-dominant company, where it was almost guaranteed that I'd never run into a co-worker with my tits out at House of Yes.

I weighed the options, knowing that there was only one logical choice, but I'd be damned if I wasn't going to be strategic about all of this. I told Insurance that Social Media had also sent me an offer (not a lie) and that the salary was twenty thousand dollars more (perhaps a little more of a lie) and tried to pit them against one another in a one-dog fight. It worked out in my favor, and though I didn't get twenty thousand dollars more, they met me in the middle, which more than solidified my decision. Michelle Ensor happily accepted the position.

It ended up being the best job I could have ever asked for. The team was great, I had access to a caring and adept C-suite who I learned so much from that I'm not sure it's measurable, and most critically, this company sent me all over the world. They had multiple offices in Asia, and I was able to travel there several times a year.

The first time I went to China I had a scheduled layover in Korea. My boss, knowing that I was adopted, suggested that I take some time to visit, even if it was only for a couple of days. She said that she'd approve a fancy hotel in the heart of Seoul so that I could expense it. She may not have known it, but she changed my life in more ways than one.

That evening after work I went to therapy, where I opined that

I didn't know whether to go or not—which, looking back, feels so very demented, but I was scared. Scared that I wouldn't like it? Scared that I would like it too much? My anxiety was at an all-time high (this was a *good* good job) and though I thought it would be the easier company to work for, I had proved myself wrong once again. Not to mention, I had fancy taste. I didn't think I'd be able to adapt to a life of ramen noodles again, at least not the kind I had in jail. I spouted all of this out to Will, my therapist, and he listened patiently. When I paused to take a breath, he shot me a look of *are you done yet?* And said something that will stick with me for the rest of my days, something I still remind myself of often.

"You have to go," he said. "It would be such a disservice to yourself if you did anything but try. And you have to leave the airport."

Will wasn't a particularly talkative guy (he nodded a substantial amount), which isn't the best quality for a therapist, so the fact that he was telling me to do *anything* put even more weight on what he was saying.

"Yeah, maybe. You could be right," I said.

Getting in the slow-ass elevator, descending to ground level, I felt my blood pressure rise. Should I? Shouldn't I? By the time we were passing the second floor I had decided not only that I should, but that I could.

When I recounted this conversation to friends, they didn't get it. They were sympathetic of course, but most of them couldn't comprehend how I would even question it, which I can't blame them for, because I was the most aware of how stupid my thought process was. But these friends weren't adopted, they hadn't been through what I had, they didn't question their existence in the same way I did. Sometimes, when one of them was complaining about their job, talking about how frustrating it was, I wanted to shake them and yell, *Do you want to know what real pressure is like?* But it's all relative, isn't it?

That night when I got home, I did the only thing I could, one of the few things that quiets the buzzing in my brain. I made a spreadsheet. Numbers are consistent, equations rarely change, and hard data is one of the only things in life that can be trusted. In a weird way I was jealous of math—envious of its ability to come to the same result in a myriad of ways. The dataset I was working with at that moment was population + rate of adoption in the eighties + square mileage of Seoul. I quickly solidified what I already knew, that even if I wanted to, finding my biological parents was near impossible. I sighed in relief. The exercise had served its purpose, and I could finally focus on the fun stuff now that I had squelched the possibility of a reunion.

My back ached. I looked at the clock and realized that I had been hunched over my computer researching, organizing, and outlining my trip for six hours. The result was a jam-packed two days that would take me on a food tour, to ancient palaces that had been standing for over 650 years, and to the Demilitarized Zone. I closed my computer at exactly 11:11, my eyes burning from staring at the glowing screen, and I made a wish: that I could keep my job at least until after this trip.

After two months of waiting, the day of my departure finally arrived. Elliot dropped me off at the international terminal at JFK. He hugged me and told me to have a great time, adding a "Seriously!" as I walked away, one step closer to what had started to feel like my destiny. I shook my head in disbelief that a few weeks ago I had considered *not* going. But the thought didn't stick for long as I entered the chaos of the airport. I was nervous, but I was ready.

Nearly twenty-four hours later I stepped off the plane at Incheon International Airport, stretched my travel-weary body (why is it that you feel so exhausted even when all you've been doing is sitting?), and took in my surroundings. I was immediately struck by the fact that everyone looked like me. I knew this would be the case, of course, but nothing could prepare me for the fact that for the very first time in my life I wasn't a minority. I wasn't the "other." I wasn't the slant-eyed chink in the schoolyard. I was exactly like everyone else.

I immediately posted a video to Snapchat of the roving crowds, weaving all around the beautiful and sleek airport, with the caption *Mom??? Dad???*

I chuckled to myself, chuffed by my own joke, when I was startled by a four-foot tower of metal that was beeping as it rolled toward me. What in the good god damn? I inspected the colorful display and it prompted me to *fill it up*. Right here in the airport? Shit, Asians really are kinky. A passerby said something to me in Korean, and after seeing the perplexed look on my face said, in perfect English: "It's for your luggage." Up until a few years ago JFK had a whole-ass terminal that was *carpeted*, and here in Seoul there were robot slaves who would haul your bags around. The future is now . . . at least in Korea.

In the car on the way to my hotel downtown, I was reminded of my first taxi ride to my Prospect Heights apartment in New York. In the same way, even though I had never been there before, it felt like home. As we drove down the highway, I talked to my driver using a translation app, and holding the phone up to his face from the back seat, I got very emotional. His expression that was reflected in the rearview mirror was one of concern and I tried to explain that I was adopted and this was my first return to the motherland. The app didn't have a proper Korean word for "adopted," so I had to say, "taken away when I was a baby." He nodded knowingly and in broken English said, "It okay, here now."

The next forty-eight hours were a whirlwind. I had set out to make the most of my time there, and despite the frigid temperatures, I walked the entire city and ate my weight in dakgangjeong, tteokbokki, bibimbap, bulgogi, and kimchi. Food can be a spaceship transporting you to different planets, it can be a time machine taking you to different eras, and it can be a warm hug enveloping you in its spicy embrace. After every meal (and a hearty burp), I felt fulfilled and sufficiently fueled for the next leg of my adventure.

I visited Gyeongbokgung Palace, the largest of the Five Grand Palaces built by the Joseon dynasty, smack in the heart of Seoul with a view of Mount Bugak. I looked down at my feet and thought about how my ancestors walked the same paths, how they stepped with purpose. I also thought about how they ran as the palace was destroyed by the Japanese in 1592 and then again in 1915.

Korea has an extremely fraught history—one that would be much better explained by someone who knows what they're talking about (go and watch a YouTube video)—but it is full of occupation, war, and colonialism. It's a place that has been destroyed and rebuilt, and destroyed and rebuilt again. In the past few decades, they have transformed from a war-torn third-world country to establishing themselves as a leader in technology, science, and fashion. In 2020, South Korea was sitting pretty with the tenth-largest economy in the world and will forever be one of the planet's greatest success stories (even if they do believe in fan death—watch another YouTube video).

I thought about my own history, how I, too, had been torn down and rebuilt, and I felt a sort of pride I had never experienced before. After the first day I returned to my hotel, exhausted and sore from walking up the steep inclines of the hilly city. I washed my face with the fancy new skin-care products I had bought at one of the hundreds of stores dedicated to them and crawled into bed. I needed to get a good night's sleep. Tomorrow, I would be traveling to North Korea.

My alarm went off at 6:30 A.M., enough time for me to get

ready and enjoy a hearty breakfast from the hotel's insane buffet (IYKYK) before I boarded the bus that would carry us to one of the most enthralling, sobering, and incredible places I have ever been.

The Demilitarized Zone—DMZ for short—was established in 1953. It divides the Korean peninsula in half, separating the North from the South, and houses the Joint Security Area, which is widely seen as a peaceful buffer zone between the two, though it feels like anything but that.

On the relatively short bus ride to NK (it's a mere thirty miles from Seoul), our guide gave us the CliffsNotes version of the fascist country's relatively short history. NK was established in 1945, at the end of WWII, and even in the present day there is great famine and distress due to the megalomania of its totalitarian dictators. Most citizens were properly brainwashed and revered the Great Leader as if he were a god (seriously, they're taught that he is a celestial being who has magic abilities), and our guide pointed out that there were people who had pierced the veil of disillusion and risked their lives (and their family's lives) to escape. This information wasn't new to most of us tourists—we actively chose to go on this excursion, after all—but hearing it from someone in such close proximity was moving.

As we neared the border, the guide told us to look out the window across the Imjin River and to pay close attention to the landscape. The South Korean side was thick with trees, as one would expect in such mountainous terrain. But suddenly, drastically, even, the land was completely razed and barren. We sat in shock as the guide explained that there were no trees because North Korean citizens had cut them all down for fuel to keep themselves warm and alive. Everyone went silent as we mourned for those people, those who had so little. Someone's phone rang, cutting through the great nothingness, and reminded us how lucky and privileged we are.

We pulled into the parking lot of our first destination, the mouth of a secret tunnel that was dug and blasted by North Korea with intent to infiltrate the South. As we stepped off the bus we were greeted by some kind of derelict carnival and the ever-prevailing sign of the tourism industry, an ATM. The tunnel was insane, plunging into the depths of the earth, a claustrophobic's worst nightmare. The decline and the subsequent incline as we traversed back up were steep, and many people were grumpy that they weren't warned. There were some who stopped halfway to catch their breath and never got back up . . . kidding, they went back to the bus early. Regardless of whether you made the entire journey, there was no question that the construction was a feat. We were told that many people died creating this vast network of tunnels that ultimately ended up not being used at all.

As we exited, sweaty and covered in dirt, we found ourselves face-to-face with yet another prevailing sign of tourism: a gift shop. It was like a dystopian Disneyland, key chains that had nothing to do with where we were (I distinctly remember a high-heeled shoe), bags of rice, and North Korean soju. I walked away with a T-shirt for Elliot and a magnet with a little soldier molded out of clay.

Our next stop was the Dorasan train station, built as a sign and hope of reunification by South Korea. It was about one thousand times nicer than Penn Station, but unlike any NYC station, it was void of commuters. The train station may as well not have existed, because it wasn't active. I sat on the comfortable seats, chin in my hand, waiting for a train to nowhere.

Our final stop was the DMZ. On the way, our guide rattled off a long list of things that were prohibited, and warned us that if we were to break the rules there was nothing he or the company could do to save us. As we arrived there were no carnival rides, there were no ATMs, there were no gift shops. We were met only by a handful of small one-story blue buildings, with scary-looking guards on both sides standing face-to-face. This is, in fact, the only place where they wouldn't be encouraged to murder one another outright.

We lined up single file and marched into one of the blue buildings, the Joint Security Area, or Truce Village. This area is beyond the jurisdiction of North and South Korea and is secured by the United Nations. It's where the leaders of both countries meet, in the rare times that they do. Inside the building we were placed in a room with a small table and a door on each side with more scary guards standing in front of them. The door across the room, marked by a single line on the floor, opened to North Korea. We were told that we could quickly step over the line, the not-so-invisible border that signified so much to so many people, so that us visitors—many, including myself, who had never known real strife—could go back to our homes and brag to our friends that we had been to North Korea.

We returned to Seoul as changed people; the bus ride back was quiet with reflection. It was an experience that would stay with me forever, one that I felt very grateful to have had. I found out a couple of days later that I had been on one of the last tours before they were shut down due to a North Korean defector who had made his way across the border, despite being shot several times, even after he had crossed into South Korea (a crime against humanity). His limp body had been dragged the rest of the way to safety, and when he finally woke up in the hospital, underneath a South Korean flag, he asked to watch TV.

I used the short time I had left on the trip to walk aimlessly around the city, reveling in the juxtaposition of the old with the new. Koreans care very deeply about preserving their history, and they've built their new world around the ancient one seamlessly. I thought about my biological mom carrying me in her womb, maybe near where I was at that very moment, and thanked her. I thought about my "real" mom and tapped out a text thanking her, too.

Sitting next to a beautiful man-made lake, teeth chattering in the cold, I cried tears of gratitude that I was here in this place at this time. My final stop, before I got back on the plane to my actual home, was to get a massage and facial. A sheet mask was applied to my entire body (!) and the kind woman who tutted at my tattoos (dishonor!) gently touched my face. The face that had features I had been mercilessly teased for throughout my life. The face that I was now so grateful for. I was truly happy to be Asian, and completely overjoyed to be Korean.

17

A WORK IN PROGRESS

I set foot on American soil for the first time in nearly a month to little fanfare. I was so tired that I couldn't think properly, and for a quick second thought that I had to get on yet another plane. With a groan, I swung my bag over to the opposite shoulder and made the far-too-long walk from the gangway to customs.

Save for those two days in Korea, I had been working in a coastal town in China that bordered the Yellow Sea. It was refreshing to be back at JFK reading signs in English that made sense (the best mistranslation from the Far East that I saw was a children's clothing store called HAPPY ASSDENT). The most exhausting part of travel is not how many miles you walk in a day, but how much overtime your brain has to put in to perform even the most basic functions.

I was thrilled to be able to navigate through the terminal to the long line for US Customs without asking for help, without any anxiety or second-guessing (*"What if someone is watching me bumble around like a dumb dick?"*).

"Welcome back," the customs agent said flatly as he stamped my passport.

I walked through the gates and sighed, both simultaneously delighted and depressed to be back in my actual homeland. This was the country that cradled my friends, my family, my enemies, my hopes and dreams, and everything I ever really knew in her arms. It's not where I was born, but it's where I was cultivated.

America, and more specifically New York City, and I will have a sordid love affair for the rest of my life. When I die, it's the sparkling halogen-lit eyes of the windows peppering the skyline that I'll think of last. The city arguably played the most pivotal role in my life; if I'm the main character, then NYC is the best supporting actor. She is a city whose reigning Lady Liberty beckons to those yearning to be free, and it feels like she actually means it. She is an insular community that is less like the nation she belongs to and more of her own planet, one that the rest of the world can only orbit around. She is a fickle bitch and she is the greatest city in the goddamn world.

"'SCUSE ME," a woman said brusquely as she shoulder-checked me on the escalator for being too slow. I smiled. It was good to be home.

I exited the airport terminal to a cavalcade of impatient honking and the smell from cigarettes being greedily inhaled. I spotted Elliot in our car, threw my suitcase in the back with as much force as I could muster, and hopped into the front seat. Leaning over, I kissed him, only a peck, as the car behind us had already started to grow impatient and was creeping up to our bumper.

"Welcome back!" Elliot exclaimed, with a lot more gusto than the customs agent.

Over the next few days I attempted to acclimate not only to the time zone, but to the hustle and bustle of the city and to the kind of culture that allows us to talk to strangers. In many other parts of the world your personal space is much more protected, and people can only balk at the idea of asking a rando how their day is going. One of my Chinese coworkers had wondered, "Why would you ask if you don't care?" I told her that in America it was rude to pretend you didn't care, and she asked, "So you just lie to everyone?" *Girl, you have no idea.*

All of my colleagues in Asia spoke English, so they understood me, but they didn't *understand* me. Early on in my trip I realized how much of my personality is wrapped up in my ability to make people laugh, and it was a shockingly isolating experience when I couldn't. All of this is to say, I was hard up for interaction.

Now back in the USA, I happily responded to catcalls with snappy retorts, I chatted up the poor MTA employee who made the mistake of sitting next to me on the train, and I *wooo'd!* for buskers in Union Square. But these interactions also brought forth a new kind of reckoning—one that I was wholly unprepared for.

Slowly, I became increasingly aware of sideways glances and

backhanded compliments (*complisults*, as I like to call them). They became easier to spot—and subsequently harder to ignore—the quiet subtexts of racial microaggressions. A couple of weeks after I got back, I was sitting in a laundromat waiting for my clothes to dry when a man approached me.

"Do you need bags?"

"Excuse me?" I was confused.

"Do you need bags to sell?" he said impatiently.

"No, I'm all good, I've got one, thanks," I said, pointing to the luggage I used to shuffle my clothes back and forth.

"That's what you sell?" he asked incredulously.

"Sell? What . . . ?"

"Yeah, to your customers."

I shook my head, my silent apology for not understanding. Then it clicked.

"Wait, do you think I work here?" I asked, my voice rising in decibels. "I don't fucking work here!"

Bag Guy looked genuinely flustered, fumbled a sorry, and hightailed it out of the store. For a moment I sat flabbergasted, and then vowed that the next time I did laundry I'd put makeup on and wear a real outfit, look more put together. (I never said that I didn't have my own racism to work on.)

Later that night on our couch, I was talking to a friend, also a Woman of Color, and I asked what the appropriate response would have been.

"To stick him in a dryer and watch him suffer," she said, "like a dog in a hot car."

"Jesus," I said as I kissed our pup in my lap on the nose, "but like . . . is it my responsibility to educate him on the intricacies of bigotry, or what?"

"I think it depends on who you ask, but if it were me I'd probably burst into tears . . . which might teach him a lesson?"

I frowned and felt like crying myself. Going to Korea, and on this larger emotional journey, was supposed to help me find myself, not confuse me further. Why did I feel so guilty for letting that guy off so easily? Shouldn't I be happy that I remained even-keeled (all things considered)? Or that I had spoken up at all? I closed my eyes tightly and wondered at what point patting yourself on the back becomes self-flagellation.

I resolved to focus on my internal growth, which meant acknowledging that I couldn't change everyone's mind—not about race, not about gender roles, not about the judicial system—only those who were open to listening. That was a hard pill to swallow, and I questioned if I was qualified to speak to anyone about anything.

On a chilly Wednesday in 2019, I was in therapy when I had what some people like to call *a breakthrough*, but what I call a mental breakdown on a five-minute break. The respite never lasts as long as you want, but you're glad you had it at all, and then it's back to work.

"Whoa, I think I realized something," I said, with bright clarity. "Every time I apologize for taking up space, or question my ability to do something I know that I can, I'm upholding misogyny and racism and the patriarchy."

My therapist nodded in agreement as I had another moment of lucidity. "And isn't it so fucked up that I have to bully myself into believing that?"

The trip to Korea, and the time in America that had passed since, spurred a newfound interest in finding myself in a way I hadn't been able to articulate before. Through all of the searching and scrambling, I had started to find my purpose: to do good in a world that had wronged me, and that I had wronged back in retaliation. I hoped that my fuckups and the lessons I had learned over the ensuing decades could serve as a cautionary tale. And most importantly, maybe I could bring light to the plight of so many of our incarcerated brothers and sisters.

For years I had donated money to and championed causes I believed in, but after I got back I started to donate more of my time as well. I got involved with amazing organizations like Black and Pink, whose advocacy is focused on formerly and currently incarcerated LGBTQIA+ members, many of whom have HIV; Books Through Bars, which pairs inmates with books that they actually want to read; and Second Chance Studios, a fellowship program that teaches formerly incarcerated individuals skills within digital media. The incredible people I've met through these organizations, and their missions, have fulfilled me in a way that at times felt like forgiveness to myself.

I now know the answer to the question I posed to my friend

after the Laundry Bag Guy incident. It's my responsibility to educate only if I want it to be. Every choice we make should be intentional, and sometimes that intent is self-preservation.

One quintessential "only in New York" evening, my friend Seth
and I went to a liquor brand's event that was legitimately cool (versus a too-crowded bar serving weak drinks with punny names and
a self-service photo booth that barely works), and not only because
some conglomerate had funneled money into it.

The night began at a swanky restaurant in Tribeca that we
didn't get to eat at. About twenty or so people milled about the
lobby, trying to sort out what was in store for us. The invitation
hadn't been very descriptive; it only alluded to the strange and mi-
raculous. Seth and I weren't expecting much, but we'll do almost
anything that's free, so we waited patiently.

Thirty minutes later we were taken into another room and split
up into groups. Each of us was given an old-school Walkman and
a cassette tape, the kind I used to record songs on from the radio,
ones so embedded in my brain that when I hear some of them
now I half expect my hometown DJ's voice to cut in. We were
instructed to put them on, and Seth gave me a *go-with-the-flow*
shrug. On the count of three we all pressed Play.

A deep alto crackled through the foam earbuds, a narrator.
The voice ushered us out of the building, and as we followed our
in-the-flesh guide, the faceless one described exactly what we were

walking by and seeing. At a corner we were instructed to look up, and after a few seconds of searching, my gaze fell upon a seemingly innocuous window of a regular-schmegular brick building. A woman gazed out, not at us, but through us, and a man appeared behind her. Perspective changed before our very eyes, and suddenly it appeared that we, the viewers, were suspended above a bed, looking down upon two lovers (or were they enemies?) who performed a beautiful dance.

I started to get emotional, not only because of the performance or the one-hundred-milligram gummy that was kicking in, but because of the power of storytelling. It sounds cheesy as fuck, but I teared up thinking about all of the hard work and coordination it took to make this one thing happen, and for a few dozen people to see it (we were out on the street, anyone could have watched, and even though I was silently begging those walking by to *look up*, no one did).

An hour later, Seth and I were being driven around in a limo that was lit by dozens of fake candles. Plastic flames "flickered" in the breeze of the open windows as we sat with what we had experienced. I felt the creative energy in my blood and on the fly told Seth that I thought my story could make for a good scripted TV show. I honestly don't know where it came from—there's a chance that when I was stoned once I had considered the idea, but it wasn't a thing I had been ruminating on—whatever the case, when I said it I meant it.

I had been contacted numerous times about doing a documentary but never really considered the requests, particularly because at that time I was still being called Michelle eight hours of the day. Going the fictional *based-on* route would give me more mental space to breathe than a documentary that I couldn't control would. Seth loved the idea (which was a seal of approval in and of itself), and we set up a meeting for the following week to start carving out a plot and writing a script.

The next few steps happened relatively quickly, at least in the scope of the Hollywood Machine. Seth introduced me to his talent managers, a ridiculously sharp group of women who ultimately became my talent managers, and we fine-tuned our pitch.

We sent the pitch out to production companies that were on our list, all big ones, many of them led by star writers, actors, and producers. My managers told me that we weren't even going to fuck with anything that wasn't top-tier. My ego was being massaged like a frat boy's at a strip club (*"you're not like the other guys"*), except that the people saying these things weren't lying to me. The reason that I know this is because no one in Hollywood would be wasting their time on an idea they didn't think they could sell, because they literally can't afford to.

The true crime genre had been on a meteoric rise, with an especially rabid lust for grifter stories. People can relate to both the predator and the prey; everyone knows what it feels like to have the wool pulled over their eyes, and everyone has wished that they could do that to someone else. Ultimately, deception is a form of survival—look to nature for hundreds of examples. We as animals toe the line of legality every day, whether it's jaywalking (technically against the law) or pretending to scan an item at the self-checkout register (obviously against the law). It happens constantly, and oftentimes these actions are rewarded. Books are written, TV shows and movies are made, and perpetrators are put on a pedestal. Clearly I fall under all of these categories, and there are people out there who will continuously parrot all of the bad things I've already thought about myself dozens of times over.

But I do wonder why it seems some people are forgiven faster than others. Men screw people over all the fucking time, and not only are they able to go on and live their lives, they're given thousands of dollars to be the keynote speaker at fancy business conferences. Men can be charged with murder and then be given record labels. And you know what? In many ways, good for them. I'm not trying to take the ability to turn their lives around away from them; quite the opposite if they are truly apologetic (and let's face it, many aren't). I wonder why they get the opportunity to do all of that, when I, and many other women, do not. I thought about this question a lot when I made the decision to move forward with the TV project.

Though I was very excited about everything that was transpiring, trying to make my dream a reality also meant marketing myself as a product, which is a slippery slope when you're talking to someone who has struggled with authenticity and now cares very much about it. As thrilled as I was, it also made me feel a little icky. But I tried to move past that, telling myself that the likelihood of this coming to fruition was slim anyway.

A few weeks after we started circulating the pitch, I received an email asking if I could be in LA in three days' time, for a meeting at Warner Brothers Studios. I told my boss that I had an "emergency," which was not *not* true, and a few hours later I was flying toward my destiny yet again (thankfully this time around not in handcuffs).

The meeting was with a brilliant woman who had several top hit shows under her stylish belt. She and her team listened intently as Seth and I talked about our vision, which was that I wanted to take control of my own narrative and that, ultimately, I wanted to bring light to the fucked-up justice system and prove that people are deserving of moving on with their lives. It was immediately clear that they understood, and they told us that they wanted to be collaborative partners.

After our meeting many, many months went by and we slowly chugged along. We were receiving positive non-update updates every few weeks, but it was a very serious exercise in patience. And the looming possibility of having my own goddamn TV show (!) made my monotonous day job feel unbearable. Every PowerPoint presentation I put together felt like torture, and oftentimes emails were written by slamming my forehead into the keyboard.

Soon, I decided I couldn't be a corporate cog in the wheel any longer. I wasn't exactly sure what I wanted to do—even if you have a successful show, you're not making piles of money; that comes with your second and third hits—but I knew that my life was not meant to be spent working for other people. I had been doing that for three decades and everyone saw how that turned out. So, I started to plan my exit.

And then the unthinkable happened. And by that, I mean the thing that countless movies, books, and scientists had warned us about and feared for so long; we had ourselves a fucking pandemic. I won't dwell on it for too long, because odds are you were affected in many ways, but sprinkled throughout the absolute horror of the situation, there were some good times mixed in, too. Our communities and families (chosen or otherwise) took care of one another. Moments of humanity kept everyone going, literally and figuratively, throughout an otherwise very bleak period. Fortunately, Elliot and I—and the majority of our friends—were, more than anything, very fucking bored.

Around this time, due to the origins of the virus, hate crimes against Asians increased by a dishearteningly and scary percentage. There had been reports that people were being attacked at the subway station that I, pre-pandemic, used every day. The worst that happened to me is that I was spat on and called names I had heard many times before. Sadly, this is very minor compared to what others were experiencing.

The more these vile acts took place and dangerous rhetoric was espoused, the prouder I became of being Asian. Because for as long as I hadn't identified as such, I came to terms that this is who I am, this is what I look like, and it doesn't have to be a burden. I had learned how to funnel the energy I spent on self-hatred into self-exploration.

And then another Black man's life was taken by those meant to protect him. Another human being, George Floyd, who had hopes and dreams not dissimilar to yours or mine, was murdered by the police. Riots, protests, kneel-ins, rallies, and marches followed. The majority of these demonstrations were peaceful (despite what the headlines said), and many were peaceful *until* the police stepped in, which subsequently brought nerve-wracking, occasionally violent standoffs between citizens and the NYPD all over the city.

As desperate and full of utter despair as the situation was, once again the community stepped up. Millions of people around the world screamed at the top of their lungs for justice while taking care of one another. Whether that was providing free water and energy bars to marchers or pouring Maalox into someone's burning eyes who had been tear-gassed, *"we keep us safe"*—a phrase chanted during protests—took many forms.

Like many others, I felt activated. Standing up for what you believe in is empowering, and I had an outlet for my anger that helped me shed the embarrassment of having been incarcerated (in some cases, dare I say I felt cool). For the first time I was able to talk about my experiences openly without judgment. And this might be my ego speaking (when is it not?), but I like to think that I did what I have always wanted to do, which is to get people to look at things in a different way.

On the flip side, it was an extremely challenging and confusing time. The sorrow of realizing there are so many things that you need to unlearn and relearn is a very difficult thing to navigate. My identity was once again stretched between being a Person of Color and being raised—for all intents and purposes—as white. It was stretched between being an abolitionist and realist (staunch believer, but it will take time), between yelling "fuck the police" and having a soft spot for the cop who unwrapped Starbursts for me while I was handcuffed in the back of the plane. Dualities are a fucking trip, and I took the time to really probe what I was told to feel at some point in my life and what I *actually* felt. And I came out of it even more confident that I was what most would consider a very good person.

Despite my desire to leave my employer, I was extremely thankful I still had my corporate job, especially when so many of my friends weren't sure what life was going to look like in a month's time. But it felt like even more of a slog than before, because I didn't feel like my work was doing any good in the world.

I thought of other ways I'd be able to make money so I could focus on my priorities. An enterprising friend of mine suggested following her lead and selling K95 masks that she had worn in her underwear to men who wanted to have a dirty little secret sitting on their faces. I considered this, and though sex work is work (and nothing to be ashamed of), I was tired of selling myself.

* * *

It took a solid fourteen months to officially pull the trigger, obsessively weighing the pros and cons, but it felt like the right kind of risk, and I finally did it. When I deleted Outlook from my phone in the lobby of my building at the end of my last day, a friend clapped and cheered me on. I'm proud to have my own media company called Without Wax Productions—a name with great meaning to me that you can read all about on the website, www.madewithoutwax.com—dedicated to uplifting and telling stories from Women of Color, across a variety of mediums. Though many projects are still in flux, every one of them is done with the mission of moving the needle toward a more compassionate society—particularly around incarceration and the judicial system, mental health, and transnational adoption—and most importantly, proving that change is possible.

When I reflect on the life that I've led thus far, I (still) don't think I can answer the question of why I did what I did. Maybe it was for control, for acceptance, for exaltation. Maybe it was to get a one-up on people who represented challenges in my life. Maybe it's because I was a kid and morality can be tricky.

I'm not sure I'll ever stop asking myself questions that are embedded in self-doubt. Am I always a good person? Am I sometimes a bad person? I'm not sure, and is anyone? The universal truth is that everyone lies; we embellish our résumés, stage our social media posts, tell our parents that we're doing fine, and often fake enthusiasm for life itself. Lying can be as fun as it is thera-peutic, and in certain situations it's a necessity. Maybe we're doing ourselves a disservice and being set up to fail (and be swindled), by not recognizing that. I don't know, I've only ever faked being a philosopher and scholar.

What I *am* sure of is that every mistake, misstep, and mis-fuck has brought me to where I am today. I've learned how to face each new challenge and opportunity with gratitude, strength, and dumb jokes about processed meat. And all of it—the good, the bad, the in-between—has made me who I am: an activist, educa-tor, kind friend, loving partner, and a good fucking storyteller. I have reclaimed my narrative, my name, and my truth as best I can. But maybe you'll never believe me.

ACKNOWLEDGMENTS

Thank-yous:

Enormous gratitude to my incredible editor, Hannah Phillips. She is patient, brilliant, kind, and always has great hair, which is incredibly important to the process. Katie Bassel, Michelle Cashman, Jessica Zimmerman, Jill Schuck, and the entire team at St. Martin's Press—so many people came together to make this book happen, it's really all of ours. Unless it doesn't sell well, in which case you can pretend this never happened.

My team, the people who bet on me as their winning horse, even when I was limping along, waiting to be sent to the glue factory. They've always believed in me, and I've never felt such unrestrained, honest support. Lily Dolin and Byrd Leavell, thank you for encouraging me to do this. Isaiah Telewoda, we on the rise, my bruh! Lauren Hochhauser, thank you for always accepting my "super quick" calls. Liz DeCesare, Jill Kaplan, and Jennie Frankel-Frisbie, you have been champions for me, my story, and my future for six years and counting, and I couldn't be more thankful.

My family and friends are the only reason that I exist. They nurture and care for me and talk a lot of shit to keep me grounded. In absolutely no particular order: John Renaud, Dalia Klausner, Lauren Appelwick, LeighAnn Loftus, Katie Klein, Vanessa Chambers, Brian Shahwan, Zack Rosenberg, Boram and Alex Brooks, Chris Dignes, Caitlin Lacroix, Liz Van Voorhis, Zach Mack, Brett Rouse, Solonje Burnett, Mary Pilon (my forever mentor), Alexis Schottenstein, Megan Mass, Sharlee Taylor, Richard Blakeley, Mistress Fae, Nikki Jason, Alison Flood, Stephanie Fuller, Oyster Kim, Jenna Blaha, Hanna Furey, Kestrin Pantera, Chelsea Devantez, Nico Pancorvo, Sam Wolf, Erick Mancebo, Carol Paik, Jennifer Wright, Sophia Le Fraga, Natasha Dubash, Graham Nolan, Mindy Kaling, Stephanie Henriques, Shanna Nash, Jerzy Mitchell, AJ Daulerio, Paul Square, Adrian Muniz, April Shih, Sara Menefee, Sarah Peters, and Mike Baker, and a special shout-out to Seth Porges for being the best collaborator and friend. To my drug dealer and the guy from the Bed-Stuy bodega, who kept me alive by giving me a great deal on bagels with butter way back when, I wouldn't be here without you. The honest truth is that there are too many people to name, and for that I'm so lucky. To the abolitionists, liberators, freedom fighters, rabble-rousers, and educators: in solidarity, forever. None of us are free until all of us are free.

Thank you to my big little brother, Kyle Ferrell, and his family; Calvin, my very patient stepfather; my loving grandparents who are no longer with us; and the Ensor fam.

Mom and Dad, I went into writing this book knowing that

ultimately it was a love letter to the two of you. Thank you for everything you have done for me. I am so glad you're my mom and dad and that you adopted me.

Elliot, there are no words other than "murder-suicide." I love you beyond measure. Thank you for making me laugh harder than anyone else ever could, all while propping me up in every way possible.

I'm Sorrys:

To anyone whom I have hurt, whether that was in a minor way or a psychologically fucked-up way, I am sorry. I hope my actions prove and continue to prove that I want something greater for everyone. I want to change people's perspectives, in hopes that others won't have to experience what I did to you and what you went through.